P9-DVN-622

ANTHOLOGY OF RENAISSANCE MUSIC

In the same series:

Anthology of Medieval Music, ed. Richard H. Hoppin
Anthology of Classical Music, ed. Philip G. Downs
Anthology of Romantic Music, ed. Leon Plantinga
Anthology of Twentieth-Century Music, ed. Robert P. Morgan

The Norton Introduction to Music History

Anthology of RENAISSANCE MUSIC

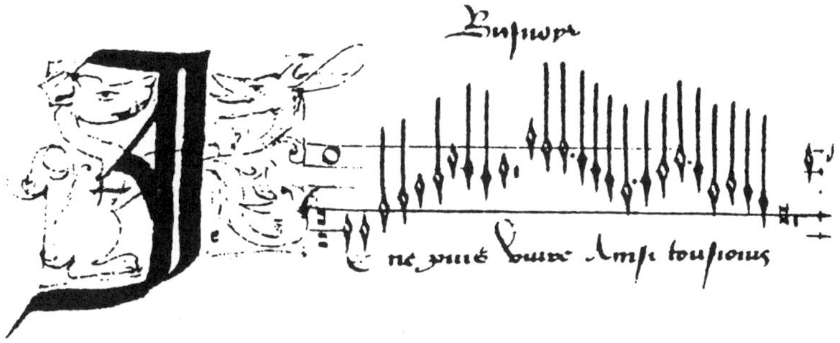

Music in Western Europe, 1400–1600

ALLAN W. ATLAS, EDITOR

Brooklyn College and the Graduate School, The City University of New York

W. W. NORTON & COMPANY
New York · London

For a discography of the works contained in this volume, visit our website at:
http://www.wwnorton.com/college/music/renmusic

Printed in the United States of America
First Edition

The text of this book is composed in Bembo
Composition and layout by Gina Webster
Manufacturing by Victor Graphics
Cover illustration: Pieter Brueghel, *Peasant Dance*, courtesy of the Kunsthistorisches Museum, Vienna

W. W. Norton & Company, Inc., 500 Fifth Avenue, New York, N.Y. 10110
http://www.wwnorton.com

W. W. Norton & Company Ltd., 10 Coptic Street, London WC1A 1PU

1 2 3 4 5 6 7 8 9 0

Contents

Preface

This anthology serves as a companion volume to *Renaissance Music*, which appears in the Norton Introduction to Music History series and contains discussions of all 102 pieces included here. It can, of course, also stand as an independent anthology, for study or performance or both. With these purposes in mind, I have tried to make the collection as all-embracing as possible: there are works from the end of the fourteenth century to the beginning of the seventeenth, from traditions both central and parallel, from genres that reflect the entire gamut of the period's musical creativity, and from composers both great and less than great. Though many of the compositions already have a secure place in the "early music" canon, some of them, at least, are less well-known.

Most of the pieces are given in their entirety, but compromises had to be struck in connection with Mass settings and other extremely lengthy works. Yet even here, Masses are represented by one or more entire movements, and Du Fay's *Missa Se la face ay pale* appears from beginning to end. Finally, English translations are provided at the back of the book for all foreign-language texts.

As I learned firsthand, the compilation and production of an anthology is a complicated task. My thanks, then, to those at W. W. Norton who helped put this one together: Michael Ochs, Martha Graedel, Susan Gaustad, and Roy Tedoff, and to Gina Webster and Kenneth Yarmey, all of whom took care of everything.

Allan W. Atlas
August 1997

ANTHOLOGY OF RENAISSANCE MUSIC

1 JOHN DUNSTABLE *Quam pulchra es*

40
45
et vi - de - a - mus si flo-res fru-ctus par - tu - ri-(er)-unt, si flo-ru-e - runt
et vi - de-a - - mus si flo-res fru-ctus par - tu - ri-(er)-unt, si flo-ru-e - runt ma-
et vi - de-a - - mus si flo-res fru-ctus par - tu - ri-(er)-unt, si flo-ru-e - runt
50
55
ma-la Pu-ni - ca. I-bi da-bo ti - bi u - be - ra me - a. Al - le - - - lu - ia.
- la Pu-ni - ca. I-bi da-bo ti - bi u - be - ra me - a. Al - le - - - lu - ia.
ma-la Pu-ni-ca. I - bi da-bo ti - bi u - be - ra me - a. Al-le - - - lu - ia.

2 JOHANNES BRASSART *Sapienciam sanctorum*

Fauxbourdon
30
35
E-xul - ta-te jus - ti in Do-mi - no:
rec - tos de- cet col-lau - da - ci - o.
Rec - tos de - cet col-lau - da - ci - o.
Glo-ri - a Pa-tri, et Fi-li - o, et Spi - ri - tu - i San - cto.
Fauxbourdon
Sic - ut e - rat in
Sic - ut e - rat in
etc.
40
45
prin - ci - pi - o, et nunc, et sem - - per, et in
prin - ci - pi - o, et nunc, et sem - - per, et in
50
55
se - cu - la se - cu - lo - rum. A - - - men.
se - cu - la se - cu - lo - rum. A - - - - men.

3 GUILLAUME DU FAY *Ave regina caelorum*

4 JOHN DUNSTABLE *Veni sancte spiritus / Veni creator*

40
45
-me, dul - cis hos - pes a - ni - me,
Pre - can - ti - bus hu - ma -
-ris, do - num De - i al - tis - si - mi,
si -
50
dul - ce re - fri - ge - ri - um.
-ni - tus sal - va nos di - vi - ni - tus
I2
55
60
In la - bo - re re - qui - es, in e - stu tem - pe-ri - es,
a ser - pen - tis fa - ci - e.
fons vi - vus, i - gnis, ca - ri - tas, et spi - ri - ta - lis un-
-ta, im - ple
65
70
in fle - tu - so - la - ti - um. O lux be - a - tis - si-
In cu - jus pre - sen - ti-
-cti - o. Tu se - pti - for - mis mu - ne - re, dex - tre De - i tu
su - per -

75
80
-ma, re - ple cor - dis in-ti - - - -
-a, ex
di - gi - tus, tu ri - te pro - mis - so Pa -
85
90
-ma tu - o - rum fi - de - li - um.
tu - a cle - men - - - ti - a
-tris, ser - mo - ne di - tans gut - tu - ra.
-na gra - - -
C
[3C]
95
Si - ne tu - o nu - - mi - ne, ni - hil est
tec - ta sint pec - ca - ta. No -
Ac - cen - de lu - men sen - si - bus, in -
II₁-tia. [-tus] Men - -
100
in lu - - - mi - ne, ni - hil est in - no - xi - um. La - va
-stra (-que) ser - vi - ti - a cor - da pe - ni -
-fun - de a - mo - rem cor - di - bus, in - fir - ma no -
-tes tu - o - rum vi - - -

105
quod est sor - di - dum, ri - ga quod est a - ri - dum,
- ten - ti - a ti - bi fac pla -
- stri cor - po - ris vir - tu - te fir - mans per - pe - tim.
si
110
sa - na quod est sau - ci - um. Fle - cte quod
- ca - ta. Lan - gui - do - rum con - so -
Ho - stem re - pel - las lon - gi - us, pa -
II2 - ta, im -
115
est ri - gi - dum, fo - ve quod est fri - gi -
- la - tor et la - pso - rum re - for - ma - tor,
- cem - que do - nes pro - ti - nus: duc - to - re sic
- ple su - per -
120
- dum, re - ge quod est de - vi - um.
mor - tis me - di - ci - na.
te pre - vi - o, vi - te - mus om - ne no - xi - um.
na gra -

125
Da tu - is fi - de - li - bus, in te con - fi - den - ti - bus,
Pec - ca - to - rum per - do - na -
Per te sci - a - mus da Pa - trem
III₁-tia. [-tus] Men - tes tu - o - rum
130
135
sa - crum se - pte - na - ri - um.
tor, e - sto no - ster ex -
nos - ca - mus at - que Fi - li - um,
vi - si -
140
Da vir - tu - tis me - ri - tum, da sa - lu - tis e - xi - tum,
pur - ga - tor, et duc
te u - tri - us - que spi - ri - tum
III₂ - ta, im - ple su - per -
145
(♯) 150
da per - en - ne gau - di - um.
ad di - vi - na.
cre - da - mus om - ni tem - po - re.
na gratia.

5 ANONYMOUS *Deo gracias, Anglia*

2 He set a siege, forsooth to say,
To Harflu town with royal array;
That town he won and made affray
That France shall rue till Domesday:
Deo gracias.

3 Then went him forth our king comely;
In Agincourt field he fought manly;
Through grace of God most marvellously
He had both field and victory:
Deo gracias.

4 There lordës, earlës and baron
Were slain and taken and that full soon,
And some were brought into London
With joy and bliss and great renown:
Deo gracias.

5 Almighty God he keep our king,
His people and all his well-willing,
And give them grace withouten ending;
Then may we call and safely sing:
Deo gracias.

6 NICOLAS GRENON *La plus jolie et la plus belle*

7 BAUDE CORDIER *Se cuer d'amant*

8 JOHANNES CICONIA *Ut te per omnes / Ingens alumnus Padue*

- dos lu - - mi - - na, Fran - ci - sce, no - stros spi - - ri -
Fran - ci - scus al - mi sup - pli - - cat
- tus. Tu qui pe - ren - - nis glo - ri - - e se - des tu -
Fran - ci - sci a - do - rans nu - mi - - na. Sis tu - tor ex - cel - - sis
- e - re om - ni - pa - tris, qui cun - cta nu - - tu con - - cu - - tit, per -
fa - - vens ser - vo pre - - can - - ti te tu - - o, quem
- ver - - sa no - bis e - ru - - e.
to - tus or - bis pre - di - - cat in - si - - gni - - bus, pre - - co - - ni -

45
- is.
50
55
60
II

65
Chri - sti le - - tus quod sum - - pse - - rat
Au - di li - - bens di - - gnas pre - - ces
70
vul - - nus re - ce - ptum per tu - - um no - bis be - ni - gne por - - ri -
doc - - to - - ris im - - men - si, sa - cer
75
80
- ge ut de te ca - nens glo - - ri - - am
Fran - ci - sce, quo le - ges bo - nas An - te - no -
85
sic il - la fe - lix re - gu - la, fra - trum mi - no - rum no - - mi - - ne,
- ris stirps ac - ci - pit. Sil - vas per al - - tas a - - li - tus,

90
cu - - jus fu - - i - - sti con - - di - - tor du - - ret per e - - vum lon - gi - - us.
in mo - le clau - sus cor - - po - ris, du - - cens vi - am ce - le - - sti - um,
95
A -
re - - ctor ve - - ni fi - - de - - li - um. A -
100
105
110
- men.
- men.

9 JOHANNES CICONIA *O rosa bella*

20
- ri - - re, Non mi las - sar mo - ri - - re, Non mi las - sar mo - ri - - re,
- to ho - ra, Vi - de che io mor' tu - - to ho - ra, Vi - de che io mor' tu - to ho - ra
Non mi las - sar mo - ri - - re, Non mi las - sar mo - ri - - re, in
Vi - de che io mor' tu - to ho - ra, Vi - de che io mor' tu - to ho - - ra per
25
in cor - te - si - - a, in cor - te - si - - a, in cor - te - si -
per que - sta iu - de - - a, per que - sta iu - de - - a, per que - sta iu - de -
cor - te - si - a, in cor - te - si - a, in cor - te - si -
que - sta iu - de - a, per que - sta iu - de - a, per que - sta iu - de -
30
35
- a.
- a.
- a.
- a.
2. Ay, ay, las - sa me, ay,
3. So -, so - co - ri - mi, so -
40
2. Ay, ay, las - sa me,
3. So -, so - co - ri - mi,
45
las - sa me, ay, las - sa me, ay las - sa me, ay las - sa me, do - len -
- co - ri - mi, so - co - ri - mi, so - co - ri - mi, so - co - ri - mi or - ma -
ay, las - sa me, ay, las - sa me, ay, las - sa me,
so - co - ri - mi, so - co - ri - mi, so - co - ri - mi

50
- te, de- - ço fi - ni - re, de - ço fi - ni - re,
- y del mio lan - gui - re, del mio lan - gui - re,
do- - len- - te, de- - ço fi- - ni- - re, de - ço fi-
or- - ma- - y del mio lan- - gui- - re, del mio lan-
55
de - ço fi - ni- - re Per ben ser - vi - - re,
del mio lan - gui- - re, Cor del cor mi - - o,
- ni - re, de - ço fi- - ni- - re Per ben ser-
- gui - re, del mio lan- - gui- - re, Cor del cor
60
per ben ser - vi - re, per ben ser - vi - - re e le - al - men - te a - ma-
cor del cor mi - o, cor del cor mi - - o, non mi las - sar pe - na-
- vi - re, per ben ser - - vi - - re, per ben ser - vi - re e le - al - men - te a-
mi - o, cor del cor mi - - o, cor del cor mi - o, non mi las - sar pe-
65
1.
2.
70
- re.
- re.
- ma-
- re.
- re.

10 JOHN DUNSTABLE OR JOHN BEDYNGHAM *O rosa bella*

35
40
- te dezo finire per ben servi - re e
del mio langui-re, cor del corpo mio, non
de - zo fi - ni - re per ben ser-vi - re
del mio lan - gui - re, cor del cor-po mio,
45
li - al - ment' a - ma - - - - re.
me las - sar mo - ri - - - - re.]
e li - al - ment' [e li - al - ment'] a - ma - - - re.
non me las - sar [non me las-sar] mo - ri - - - re.]

11 GUILLAUME DU FAY *Resvellies vous et faites chiere lye*

Ce vous con - vient ung chas - cum fai - re fe - ste, Pour bien grig -
nier la bel - le com-pagny - - - e;
Char - le gen - til,
Char - le gen - til,
Char - le gen - til,
c'on dit de Ma - le-tes-
-te.

1. Il a dame belle et bonne choysie,
   Dont il sera grandement honnourés;
2. Car elle vient de tres noble lignie
   Et de barons qui sont mult renommés.
3. Son propre nom est Victoire clamés;
   De la colonne vient sa progenie.
   C'est bien rayson qu'a vascule requeste
   De cette dame mainne bonne vie.
   Charle gentil, c'on dit de Maleteste.

12 GUILLAUME DU FAY *Adieu m'amour, adieu ma joye*

13 GILLES BINCHOIS *Dueil angoisseus*

FOR 3 VOICES

45
-rir ne mo- -rir.

FOR 4 VOICES

Dueil angoisseus
lango sans fin
Tenor
Contratenor concordans
sequenti
Contratenor concordans
Dueil an - gois - seus, ra - ge de me - seu - ré - - - -
Lan - gor sans fin et vie - e ma - leu - ré - - - -
Ct. conc.
Ct. conc. sequ.
8
- - e, Grief des-es - poir plain de for - ce - [ne] - ment,
- - e Plai - ne de plour d'an - gois - se et de - tor - - ment
1.
2.
17
Coeur do - lo - reux

2. Fierté, durté de joye separée,
Triste penser, parfont gemissement,
Angoisse grant en las cuer enserrée,
Courroux amer porté couvertement,
Morne maintien sanz resjoössement,
Espoir dolent qui tous biens fait tarir,
Si song en moy, sanz partir nullement;
Et si . . .

3. Soussi, anuy qui tous jours a durée,
Aspre veillier, tressaillir en dorment,
Labour en vain, a chiere alangourée,
En grief travail infortunément,
Et tout le mal, qu'on puet entierement
Dire et penser sanz espoir de garir,
Me tourmentent desmesurément;
Et si . . .

4. Princes, priez a Dieu qui bien briefment
Me doint la mort, s'autrement secourir
Ne veult le mal ou languis durement;
Et si . . .

14 GUILLAUME DU FAY *Nuper rosarum flores*

plum ma - chi - næ Con-de - co - ra - runt per - - pe - tim. 2. Ho - di - e
Gran - dis templum ma - chi - næ Con- de - co - ra-runt per - pe - tim.
vi-ca-ri-us Je-su Chri-sti et Pe - - - tri Suc - ces - sor Eu -
2. Ho - di-e vi - ca-ri-us Je - su Christi et Pe - tri Suc - ces - sor Eu -
imitation
word painting
ge - ni - us Hoc i - dem am - plis - si - mum Sacris templum ma-ni -
ge - ni - us Hoc i - dem am - plis-simum Sa-cris templum mani-bus San - -
n bus San - ctis - que li - quo - ri - bus
ctis -que li - - quo - ri - bus
Con - se-cra - - re di - gna - tus est.
Con - se - cra - re di - - gna - tus est.

3. I - - - gi - tur, al - ma pa - - - rens Na -
3. I - - gi - tur, al - - ma pa - - - - rens Na -
- - ti tu - i et fi - li - a, Vir - - -
- - ti tu - i et fi · - li - a, Vir - - - - -
- go de - - cus vir - gi - num, Tu - us te Flo - ren - ti -
- go de - cus vir - gi - num, Tu - us te
ae De - - - - vo - tus o - rat po - pu - lus,
Flo - ren - ti - ae De - vo - - tus o - rat po - - pu-lus,
Ut qui men - te et cor - po - re
Ut qui men - te

105
110
Mun - do quic - - - - quam ex - - o - ra - rit
et cor - po - re Mun - do quic - quam ex - o - ra - rit
25
26
27
28
115
120
4. O -
4. O -
III,1
2
3
4
5
6
7
8
9
125
130
- - - - - - ra - ti - o - ne tu - - a Cru - ci - a -
- - - - - - ra - ti - o - ne tu - a Cru -
10
11
12
13
14
15
16
17
18
135
140
tus et me - - ri - tis Tu - - i se - cun - dum car - nem
ci - a - tus et me - ri - tis Tu - i se - cun - dum car - nem
19
20
21
22
23
24
25
26
27
28
145
Na - - - - - ti do - mi - ni su - -
Na - - - - - ti do - mi - ni su -
IV,1
2
3
4
5

150
- - i
- - i
6
7
8
9
10
155
Gra - - -
11
12
13
14
15
160
- - - ta be - ne - fi-ci - a
Gra - ta be - ne - fi - ci - a
16
17
18
19
20
165
Ve - ni - am - que re - a - tum Ac -
Ve - ni-am - que re - a - tum Ac - ci - pe -
21
22
23
24
25
170
ci - - pe - re me-re - a - - tur. A - - - - men.
re me - re - - a - tur. A - - - - men.
A - - - - men.
A - - - - men.
26
27
28

15 GUILLAUME DU FAY *Ave regina caelorum* (III)

X = CF

25
tu - i la - ben - - tis Du - fa - - - - - y,
tu - i la - ben - - tis Du - fa - - - - - y, Ne
re - gi - na cae - lo - - - - rum,
tu - - i la - ben - tis Ne
30
35
Ne pec - ca - to - - - rum, ru - at in i - -
pec - ca - to - rum ru - at in i - - gnem
A - - - ve do - mi -
pec - ca - - to - rum ru - - - at in i - -
40
- - gnem fer - vo - - - - - - - - -
fer - co - - - - - - - - - -
na an - ge - lo - - - - - -
- - - gnem fer - vo - - - - - - - - - - - -
45
- - - rum. Sal - - - ve ra - - -
- - - - - rum. Sal - - - - ve ra - - - -
- - - rum. Sal - - - - -
- - - rum. Sal - - - - - -

50
dix san - cta, Ex qua mun - - do lux est
dix san - - - cta, Ex qua mun - - - do lux est
ve ra - - dix san - - cta,
ve ra - dix san - cta, Ex qua mun - do lux
55
60
or - - - ta, Mi - se - re - re, mi- se - re - -
or - - ta, Mi - se - re - re, mi - se- re - -
est or - ta, Mi - se - re - re, mi- se - re - re,
65
re, ge - ni - trix Do - - - mi- ni, Ut pa - -
re, ge - ni - trix Do - mi - ni, Ut pa - te- at por - -
Ex qua
ge - ni - trix Do - mi - ni,
70
te - at por - - - - - ta cae - - - - -
- ta cae - - - - - -
mun - - - - - do lux est
Ut pa - te - at por - ta cae - - - - -

75
li, de - bi - li.
li de - bi - li, de - bi - li.
or - ta.
li de - bi -li, de - bi - li.
80
Gau - de glo - ri - o - sa, su - per o - mnes spe - ci -
Gau - de glo - ri -
Gau - de glo - ri - o - sa, su - per o - mnes
85
90
o - sa, Mi - se - se - re, mi - se - re - re sup - pli - can -
Mi - se - se - re, mi - se - re - re sup - pli -
o - sa,
spe - ci - o - sa, Mi - se - re - re, mi - se - re sup - pli - can -
95
ti Du - fa - y Sit - que in con -
can - ti Du - fa - y Sit - que in
su - per
ti Du - fa - y Sit - que

100
105
spe - ctu tu - o mors e - jus spe - ci - - o - - -
con - spe - ctu tu - - o mors e - jus spe - - ci - - o -
o - - - - - mnes spe - ci - - o - - -
in con - spe - ctu tu - o mors e - - jus spe - ci-
110
- - - - sa. Va - - - - - - le val - de de - co - -
- - - sa.
sa. Va - - - -
o - - sa. Va - - - - - - le, val - de
115
120
- - - - ra, Et pro no - - - bis sem - - - per Chri-
sem - - - per
- - - le,
- - co - - ra, Et pro no - - bis
125
- - - - stum ex - - o - - - - ra In ex - cel - sis
Chri - - - stum ex - o - - - - ra, In ex - cel - sis
val - - - -
In ex - cel - sis

130
ne da-mne - - - mur, mi-se - - re - re no - bis Et ju -
ne da-mne - - mur. mi - se - re - re no - - - bis Et
de de - co - - - - ra,
ne da - mne - mur. mi-se-re-re no - bis Et
135
140
- - - va, ut in
ju - - va, ut
ju - - - - - va, ut in mor -
145
mor - - - - - - - tis ho - - - - - - -
in mor - - - - - - tis ho - - - - -
- - - - - - - - - - - - tis ho -
150
- - - - - - - - - - ra No - -
- - - - - - - - - - ra
Et pro
- - - - - - - - - - ra

155
stra sint cor-
sint
no- bis sem-per Chri- stum ex- o-
No- stra sint
160
cor-
cor-
165
da de-co- ra.
da de-co -ra.
ra.
da de-co -ra.
170

16 LEONEL POWER *Missa Alma redemptoris mater:* Gloria and Credo

GLORIA

35
ce - le - stis de - us pa - ter om - ni-po - tens. Do - mi - ne fi -
de - us rex ce - le - stis de - us pa - ter om - ni - po - tens. Do - mi - ne
42
- li u - ni - ge - ni - te ihe - su chri - -
fi - li u - ni - ge - ni - te ihe - su chri -
per - - - vi -
49
- ste. Do - mi - ne de - us a - gnus de - i fi - li - us pa - -
- ste. Domi - ne de - us a - gnus de - i fi - li - us pa - -
- - a ce - - li
56
- - - - tris. Qui tol - lis pec - ca - ta mun - di
- - tris. Qui tol - lis pec-ca - ta mun - di
por - - - - - - - -
63
mi-se - re-re no - bis. Qui tol - lis pec - ca - ta mun - di su - - - -
mi - se - re-re no - bis. Qui tol-lis pec - ca - ta mun - di su - -
- ta ma - - - - - - nens,

70
- sci - pe de - pre - ca - ci - o - nem no - stram. Qui se - des ad dex - te - ram pa -
- sci - pe de - pre - ca - ci - o - nem no - stram. Qui se - des ad dex - te - ram patris
Et stel - - -
77
- tris mi - se - re - re no - bis. Quo - ni - am tu so - lus san -
mi - se - re - re no - bis. Quo - ni - am tu so - lus san - -
- la ma - - ris suc - cur - re ca - den - - -
84
- ctus. Tu so - - lus do - mi - nus. Tu so - lus
- ctus. Tu so - lus do - mi - nus. Tu so - lus
- tis sur - - -
90
al - tis - si - mus. Ihe - su chri - ste cum san - cto spi - ri - tu in
al - tis - si - mus. Ihe - su chri - ste cum san - cto spi - ri - tu in
- ge - re
90
glo - ri - a de - i pa - - tris. A - - - men.
glo - ri - a de - i pa - - tris. A - - men.]
qui cu - rat po - pu - lo.]

CREDO

Pa - - - - - - - - trem om -
Pa - - - - - - - trem
[Tenor TACET]
- ni - po - ten - tem. Fa - cto - rem ce - li et ter -
om - ni - po - ten - tem. Fa - cto - rem ce - li et ter -
- re vi - si - bi - li - um om - - ni - um et in -
- re vi - si - bi - li - um om - ni - um et in -
- vi - si - bi - li - um. Et in u - num do - - mi - num ihe - sum
- vi - si - bi - li - um. Et in u - num do - mi - num ihe - sum
chri - - stum fi - li - um de - i u - - ni -
chri - - stum fi - li - um de - i u - - ni -
- ge - ni - tum. Et ex pa - tre na - tum an - te
- ge - ni - tum. Cru - ci - fi - xus e - ci - am pro no -
Tenor
Al - - - - - - - - -

43
om - ni - a se - cu - la. De - um de de - o lu - men de
- bis sub pon - ci - o pi - la - to pas - sus et se - pul - tus est. Et
- - - - ma [re - demp - to - -
51
lu - mi - ne de - um ve - rum de de - o ve - ro.
re - sur - re - xit ter - ci - a di - e se - cun - dum scrip - tu - ras et a -
- - - - ris
59
Ge - ni - tum non fa - ctum con - sub - stan - ci - a - lem pa - tri per quem om -
- scen - dit in ce - lum se - det ad dex - te - ram pa - - - tris. Et i -
ma - ter,
67
- ni - a fa - - cta sunt. Qui prop - ter nos ho - mi -
- te - rum ven - tu - rus est cum glo - ri - a iu - di - ca - re vi -
que
75
- nes et prop - ter no - stram sa - lu - tem de - scen - dit de ce - lis. Et
- vos et mor - tu - os. Cu - ius re - gni non e - rit fi - -
per - -

83
in - car - na - tus est de spi - ri - tu san - cto ex ma - ri - a vir - gi - ne et ho -
- nis et in spi - ri - tum san - ctum do - mi - num et vi -
- - vi - a ce - -
91
- - - - mo fa - ctus est. Qui ex pa - - -
- vi - fi - can - tem. Qui ex pa - - - -
- li por - -]
99
- tre fi - li - o - que pro - ce - - - - dit
- tre fi - li - o - que pro - ce - - - - dit
(por) -
105
qui cum pa - tre et fi - li - o si - mul a - do -
qui cum pa - tre et fi - li - o si - mul a - do -
- - - - ta ma - - -
111
- ra - tur et con - glo - ri - fi - ca - tur. Qui lo - cu - tus est per pro - phe -
- ra - tur et con - glo - ri - fi - ca - tur. Qui lo - cu - tus est per pro -
- - - nens,

117
- tas et u - nam san - ctam ca - - - tho - - - li - cam et
- phe - tas et u - nam san-ctam ca - tho - li - cam et
Et stel - - la
123
a - po - sto - li - cam ec - cle - si - am. Con - fi-te-or u-num bap - tis -
a - po - sto - li - cam ec - cle - si - am. Con - fi - te - or u - num bap -
ma - - ris suc - cur - re ca - den - -
129
- ma in re - mis - si-o - nem pec - ca - to - rum et ex - spe - cto
- tis - ma in re - mis - si-o - nem pec - ca - to - rum et
- ti sur - - -
135
re-sur-re - - cti - o - nem mor - tu - o - - rum.
ex - spe - cto re - sur - re - cti - o - nem mor - - - - tu - o - rum.
- ge - re
141
Et vi - tam ven - tu - ri se - cu - li. A - - - - men.
Et vi - tam ven - tu - ri se - cu - li. A - - men.
qui cu - rat [po - pu - lo.]

17 ANONYMOUS *Missa Caput:* Sanctus

35
- - us Sa - ba - - - - - -
de - - - us Sa - ba - - -
40
45
- - - - - - - - - - - - oth.
- - - - - - - - - - oth.
50
55
Ple - ni sunt cæ - li
Ple - ni sunt cæ - li
Pleni sunt
60
et ter -
et ter -

65
70
ra glo - ri - a
ra glo - ri - a
tu - a.
tu - a.
75
80
O - san -
O - san - na
Osanna
Osanna
na in ex - cel -
in ex - cel -
85
90
sis.
sis.
Be - ne - di -
Be - ne - di -
95

100
ctus qui
ctus qui
105
110
ve
ve
in nomine
in nomine
115
nit in no mi
nit in no mi ne
120
ne do mi
do mi

125
130
ni.
O -
ni.
O
san
135
san
na
na
140
145
in
ex -
in
ex - cel
150
cel
sis.
sis.

18a GUILLAUME DU FAY *Se la face ay pale*

CHANSON

Se ay pesante malle
De dueil a porter,
Ceste amour est male
Pour moy de porter;
Car soy deporter
Ne veult devouloir,
Fors qu'a son vouloir
Obeisse, et puis
Qu'elle a tel pooir,
Sans elle ne puis

C' est la plus reale
Qu'on puist regarder,
De s' amour leiale
Ne me puis guarder,
Fol sui de agarder
Ne faire devoir
D'amours recevoir
Fors d'elle, je cuij;
Se ne veil douloir,
Sans elle ne puis.

18b GUILLAUME DU FAY *Missa Se la face ay pale*

I. KYRIE

Canon: Tenor crescit in duplo.

25
30
Ky - ri - e e -
e
lei - son,
Ky - ri - e
35
lei - son.
e - lei - son.
Ky - ri - e e - lei - son.
e - lei - son.
B
40
Chri - ste e - lei -
Contra
Chri - ste e - lei -
Tenor bassus
son. Chri-
son. Chri - ste e - lei - son.
Chri - ste e - lei - son.

ste
e
Chri ste e
lei son. Chri ste
e lei son.
Chri ste
e lei son.
lei son. Chri ste e lei son.
C
Ky ri e
e
Ky ri e
e
Ky ri e
Ky ri e
e
lei son. Ky ri e
lei son.
e lei son.
Ky ri e
e
lei son.

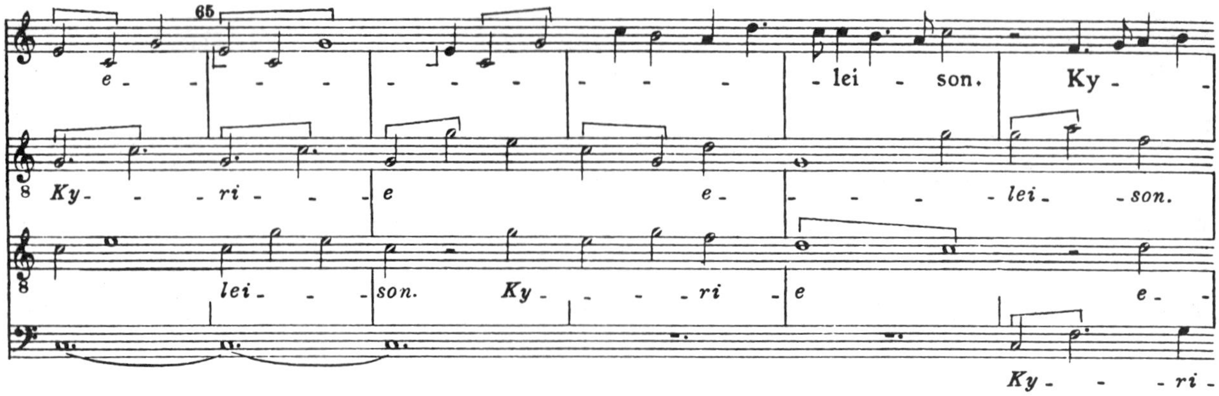

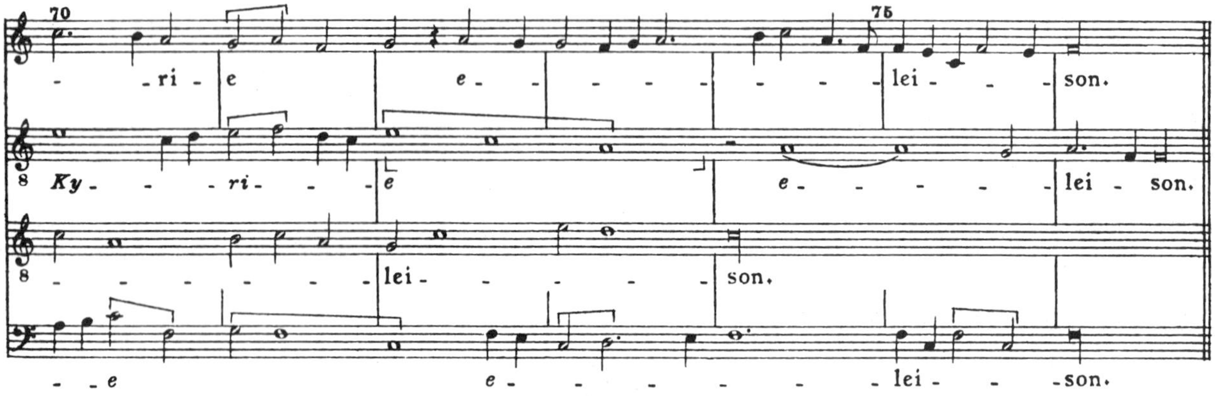

II. GLORIA IN EXCELSIS DEO

Canon: Tenor ter dicitur. Primo quælibet figura crescit in triplo, secundo in duplo, tertio ut jacet.

15
tis. Lau - da - - mus te. Be - ne - di - ci -
tis. Lau - da - - - - - - mus te. Be - ne - di - ci - mus
20
mus te. Ad - o - - - ra -
te. Ad - o - ra - mus te. Glo - ri - fi -
Ad - - - - - o - - - ra - - - - - - - - mus
Ad - o - - - - - - - - - - - ra - mus te.
25 30
mus te. Glo - ri - fi - ca - - - mus
ca - - mus te. Gra -
te. Glo - - - - - - ri - - fi - - - - - -
Glo - ri - - - - - - - - - - - - - - - -
35
te. Gra - ti - as a - gi -
ti - as a - gi - mus ti - - bi pro - pter ma - gnam
ca - - - - - - - mus te.
fi - - - ca - mus te. Gra - ti - as

mus ti bi pro - pter ma - - - gnam
Glo - ri - am tu - - - am.
Gra - - - - - - ti - - - as a - - -
a - - - - - gi - mus
glo - ri - am tu - - - - - am. Do - - - - mi -
Do - mi - - - - - - - - - -
gi - - mus ti - - bi.
Do - mi - - - - - - -
ne de - - us, rex cae - le - stis, de - us
ne de - - - us, rex cae - - - - - le - - -
Do - - mi - ne de - us, rex
- - - ne de - - - us, *rex cae - -*
pa - - - - ter o - - - mni - - po - - tens.
stis, de - - - us
cae - - - le - - - - - stis, de -
le - - - - - - - - - - - - - - stis,

65
Do - - - mi - - -
pa - - - ter o - - - mni - po - - tens.
us pa - - - ter o - mni - po - tens. Do -
de - us pa - - - - - - - - ter o - - mni - po -
70
ne fi - - - - - li
Do - - - - - mi -
mi - - - ne fi - - - li
tens. Do - mi - - - - - - - -
75
ne fi - - - - - - li u - ni - ge -
- - - - - - - - - ne fi - - li u - ni -
80
u - ni - ge - ni -
- - - - - - - - - - - - ni - te
Je - - - - - - su
ge - - - - - - - - - - - ni - - te Je - su

te Je - - su Chri - - -
Je - - - - - - - su
Chri - - - - - - - - - - ste.
Chri - - - - - - - - - ste. Do - -
- - - - - - - - - - - - - - ste. Do - - mi -
Chri - - - - ste. Do - - - - mi - - - - - -
Do - mi - ne de - - - - - - - - -
- - - mi - - - - - - - ne de - - - - - -
ne de - - us, a - - - - - gnus
ne de - - - - - - us, a - - - - - - - - - gnus de -
- - - - - us, a - - - - - - - - - - -
- us, a - - - - - - - gnus de - - - - -
de - - - i, fi - - - - -
- - - - i, fi -
gnus de - - - - - - - - i, fi - -
i, fi - - - - - - - -

110
li - us pa -
li - us pa -
li - us pa -
li - us pa -
115
tris.
tris.
tris.
tris.
B
Qui tol - lis pec -
Qui tol -
120
ca - ta mun - di, mi - se - re - re no -
lis pec - ca - ta mun - di, mi - se -
125
bis. Qui tol - lis pec - ca - ta mun -
re - re no - bis. Qui
mi - se - re - re no - bis. Qui
Qui tol - lis pec - ca - ta

130
di, su - sci - pe de - pre - ca - ti -
tol - lis pec - ca - ta mun - di, su - sci - pe
tol - lis pec - ca - ta mun - di, su - sci -
mun - di, su -
135
o - nem no - stram.
de - pre - ca - ti - o - nem no - stram.
pe de - pre - ca - ti - o - nem no - stram. Qui se -
sci - pe de - pre - ca - ti - o - nem
Qui se - des ad dex - te - ram pa - tris,
Qui se - des ad dex - te - ram pa - tris, mi - se - re - re
des ad dex - te - ram pa - tris, mi - se -
no - stram.
140
mi - se - re - re - no - bis.
no - bis, Quoni - am tu so -
re - re no - bis.
mi - se - re - re no - bis. Qvo - ni - am tu so -

145
Quo-ni-am tu
lus san- ctus. Tu so- lus
Quo- ni am
lus san- ctus.
so- lus san- ctus. Tu so- lus do- mi-nus.
150
do- mi- nus.
tu so-lus san- ctus. Tu so-lus do- mi-
Tu so- lus do- mi-nus. Tu so-
Tu so- lus al- tis- si- mus,
Tu so- lus al- tis- si- mus,
nus. Tu so- lus al- tis-si- mus, Je-
lus al-tis- si- mus, Je-
155
Je- su Chri- ste.
Je- su Chri- ste.
su Chri- ste.
su Chri- ste.

C
160
165
Cum
Cum san - - - - - - - cto spi - - - ri - tu
Cum san -
Cum san - cto spi - - - - - - - ri - - - - - - - tu
170
san - cto spi - ri - - tu in glo - - ri -
cto spi - - - - ri - tu in glo - - - - - ri -
in glo - - ri -
175
a de - - - - - - - - - i
in glo - ri - a de - - i pa - - -
a, glo - ri - a de - i pa - - - - - tris, in glo - - ri -
a de - - - - - - - i
180
185
pa - - - - tris. A - - - - - -
- - - - - - - - - tris. A - - - - - -
a de - i pa - - - - tris. A -
pa - - - - - - - - - - - - - - tris. A - - -

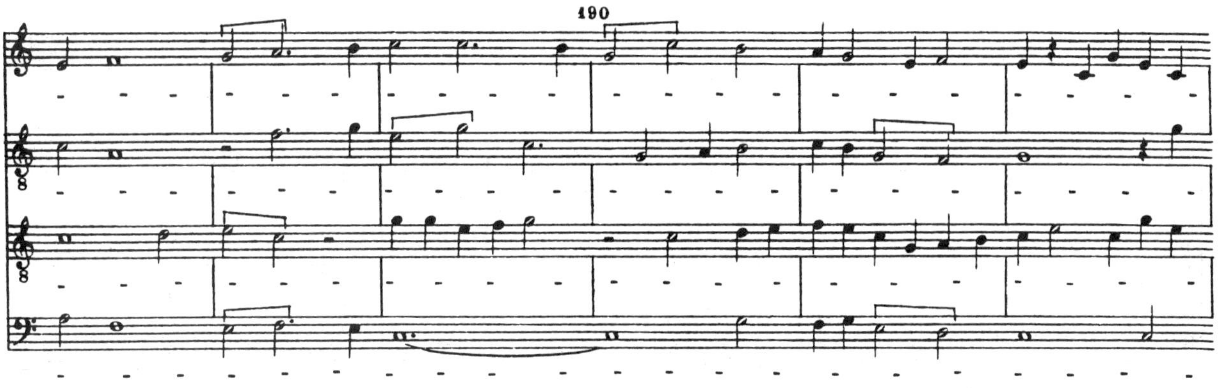

III. CREDO IN UNUM DEUM

Canon: Tenor ter dicitur. Primo quaelibet figura crescit in triplo, secundo in duplo, tertio ut jacet.

15
ter- - - - rae, vi - si - bi - li - um o- - - - mni- -
et ter- - - rae, vi - si - bi - li - um o- - - - - - - - - - mni- -
20
um et in - vi-si-bi-li-um. Et in u - num do-mi-num Je - sum Chri-stum, fi-li - um
um et in- -vi - si- -bi- -li- -um. Et
et in- - - vi- - - - - - - - si- - - -
et in- - - - - - - - - vi- - - si- - bi- - - -
25
30
de - i u - ni - ge - ni - tum. Et ex pa - tre na- - -
in u - num do - mi-num Je - sum Christum, fi - li - um de- -
bi- - li- - -um. *Et in* -
li - um. Et in u- -num do - mi- - -num Je- - -
35
- - -tum an-te o - mni - a sae- - cu - la. De - um de de - o, lu- -
i u-ni - ge - ni - tum. *Et ex pa - tre na-* -
u- - - - - num do- - - mi- - - num
sum Chri-stum, fi - li-um de - i u - ni- -

40
men de lu - mi - ne, de - um ve - - - rum de de - - - o
tum an - te o - mni - a sæ - - cu - la. De - um de de -
de - - - - - - - um ve - - - - - - - - - rum
ge - - ni - - - tum. Et ex pa - - - tre
45
ve - - - ro. Ge - ni - tum, non fa - ctum, con sub - stan - ti -
o, lu - - men de lu - mi - ne, de - um ve - - -
de de - o ve - - - ro.
na - tum an - - - - - - - - te o - - - mni - a sae - cu -
50
a - - lem pa - - tri: per quem o - mni - a fa - cta sunt. Qui propter nos ho -
rum de de - o ve - ro. Ge - ni - tum, non fa - ctum, con -
per quem o - - - mni - a fa -
la.
55
60
mi - nes et pro - pter no - stram sa - lu - tem de - scen - dit de cæ - lis.
sub - stan - ti - a - lem pa - - - tri: per quemo - mni - a fa -
- - - - cta sunt. Qui
Qui pro - - - pter

65
Et in - car - na - tus est de spi - ri - tu san - cto ex Ma - ri - - a
cta sunt. Qui pro - - - pter nos ho - mi - nes et
pro - - - - - - - pter nos ho - mi - nes et
nos ho - - - - - mi - nes et
70
vir - gi - ne: et ho - mo fa - ctus est.
pro - pter no - stram sa - - lu - - tem de - - - scen - dit
pro - - - pter no - - - - stram
pro - pter no - stram sa - - lu - - tem de - - - - -
75
de cæ - - - lis. Et in - car - na - tus est de
scen - dit de cae - lis. Et in - car - na - tus est
80
spi - - - - - ri - tu san - cto et ho - - mo fa - ctus
et ho - - - -
de spi - ri - tu san - cto et ho - - - mo

85
90
Cru - ci - fi - xus e - ti - am pro no - bis: sub Pon - ti - o Pi -
est. Cru - ci - - fi - xus
mo fa - - - - - ctus est.
fa - - - - - - - - ctus est.
95
la - - to pas - sus et se - pul - tus est. Et re - - sur -
e - ti - am pro no - bis: sub Pon - ti - o Pi - la - to
Cru - ci - fi - - - xus sub Pon - ti -
100
re - - xit ter - - ti - a di - - - - - e se - - cun - - -
pas - sus et se - pul - tus est. Et re - sur -
o Pi - - la - - to pas - sus et se - pul - tus
Et re - sur - re - xit
105
dum scri - ptu - - ras. Et a - - scen - dit in cæ - - -
re - xit ter - ti - a di - - - - - - e se - cun - dum scri - - -
est. Et a - - scen - - - dit in
ter - ti - a di - e. Et a - scen - dit in

110
lum, se - det ad dex - te - ram pa - - - - -
ptu - - ras. Et a - scen - dit in cæ - lum, se - det ad
cae - lum, se - det ad dex - te - - ram pa - - -
cae - lum, se - - det ad dex - - - - - te - - - -
115
- - - - - - - - - - - tris.
dex - te - ram pa - - - - - tris.
tris.
ram pa - - - - - - - - - tris.
B
Et i - te - rum ven -
Et i - te - rum
120
tu - rus est cum glo - - ri - a, ju - di - ca - re vi - - vos et mor - tu -
ven - tu - rus est cum glo - ri - a, ju - di - ca - re vi - vos et
- - - - - os: cu - jus re - gni non e - rit fi - - nis.
mor - tu - os: cu - jus re - - gni non e - rit fi - - - -
cu - - jus re - - gni non e - - -
cu - - jus re - gni non e - rit
125

130
Et in spi - ri - tum sanctum, do - mi - num et vi - vi - fi - can - tem:
nis. Et in spi - ri - tum san - ctum, do - mi-num et vi - vi -
rit fi - - - - - - nis. Et in
fi - - - - - - nis.
qui ex pa - tre fi - li - o-que pro - ce - - dit.
fi - can - - tem: *qui ex pa - - tre,* qui
spi - - - ri - tum san - - - ctum,
Qui cum pa -
135
Qui cum pa - tre et fi - li - o si - mul
ex pa - tre fi - li - o - que pro - ce - - dit. Qui
do - mi - num et vi - vi - fi - can - - -
tre et fi - - - - li - o si - mul
140
ad - o - - ra - - tur et con - glo - ri - fi - ca - - - -
cum pa - tre et fi - li - o si - mul ad - o - - ra - -
tem. *Qui cum pa - tre et fi - li - o ad -*
ad - o - ra - tur et con - - - - -

tur:
tur et con - glo - ri - fi - ca - tur:
o - ra - tur:
glo - ri - fi - ca -
145
qui lo - cu -
qui lo - cu - tus est per pro -
qui lo -
tur: qui lo - cu - tus est per pro -
tus est per pro - phe -
phe -
cu - tus est per pro - phe - tas.
phe - tas.
150
tas. Et u - nam san - ctam ca - tho - li - cam et
tas. Et u -
Et u - nam san - ctam ca - tho - li - cam
Et u - nam san - ctam ca - tho - li - cam

155
a- po- sto- li- cam ec-
nam san- ctam ca- tho- li- cam et a- po- sto-
et a- po- sto- li- cam ec- cle-
et a- po- sto- li-
C
160
cle- si- am. Con- fi- te-
li- cam ec- cle- si- am. Con-
si- am.
cam ec- cle- si- am.
165
or u- num bap- tis- ma
fi- te- or u- num bap- tis- ma
Con- fi- te- or u- num
Con- fi- te- or u-
170
in re-
in re- mis- si- o- nem pec- ca- to- rum.
bap- tis- ma in re- mis- si- o- nem
num bap- tis- ma in re- mis- si- o- nem pec-

175
mis-si-o-nem pec-ca-to-rum. Et ex-spe-
Et ex-spe-cto re-sur-re-cti-o-nem
pec-ca-to-rum. Et ex-spe-cto re-sur-re-cti-o-nem mor-
ca-to-rum. Et ex-spe-cto re-sur-
180
cto re-sur-re-cti-o-nem mor-tu-o-
mor-tu-o-rum.
tu-o-rum. Et
re-cti-o-nem mor-tu-o-rum. Et vi-tam ven-
185
rum. Et vi-tam ven-tu-ri sae-cu-li. A-
Et vi-tam ven-tu-ri sae-cu-li. A-
vi-tam ventu-ri sae-cu-li. A-
tu-ri sae-cu-li. A-
190
men.
men.
men.
men.
195

IV. SANCTUS

Canon: Tenor crescit in duplo.

80
- ba - - - - - - - - - - - - - - - - oth.
Sa - ba - - oth.
- ba - - - - - - - - - - oth.
- ba - - - - - - - - - - - - - - - - - - oth.
B
35
Ple - - - - - - - ni
Contra
Ple - - - - - - - - - - - - - - - ni
Tenor bassus
40
sunt cae - - - - - - - - - - - li et ter - - - -
sunt cae - - - - - - - - - - li et
45
50
- - - - - - - - - ra glo - - - - - - - - - - - -
ter - - - - - - ra
glo - - - - - - - - - - - - - - -
55
- - - - - - - - - - - ri - a
glo - - - - - - - - - -
- - - - - - - - - - - - ri - - a, glo - - - - - - - - - - - -

60
65
tu
ri
a
tu
ri
a
tu
70
a.
a.
a.
C
75
O
san
O
san
O
san
na
O
san
80
na
in
ex
na
in
ex
na
in

85
90
cel - - - - - - - - - - - - - - - - - sis.
in ex - - - - - cel - - - - - - - - - - - - - - - - sis.
cel - sis.
ex - - - - - - cel - - - - - - - - - - - - - - sis.
D
Contra
Tenor bassus
Be - ne - - - - di - - - - - - - ctus qui
Be - - - - - - - - ne - di - - - - ctus qui
95
ve - - - - - - - - - - - - - - nit
ve - - - - - - - - - - - - - nit
100
in no - - - - - - - - - -
in no - - - - - - - - - - - - -

105
mi
ne
mi
ne
do
do
110
do
mi
mi
mi
115
ni.
ni.
ni.
E
3×2/4
O
san
O
san
O
san
na
O
san

V. AGNUS DEI

Canon: Tenor crescit in duplo.

10
i qui tol- -lis pec- -ca-
-i qui
A- -gnus de-
A- -gnus de- -i
15
-ta mun-
tol- -lis pec- -ca-
-i
qui tol- -lis
20
-di,
-ta mun-
qui tol-
pec- -ca- -ta mun-
25
30
mi - se - re- -re no-
di, mi- se- -re-
lis pec- -ca - ta mun-
di, mi- -se- -re-

35
-re no-
di, mi-se-
-re
40
bis.
bis.
re-re no-
bis.
no-
bis.
B
A- gnus
Contra
A- gnus de- i
Tenor bassus
45
de- i qui tol-
qui tol- lis pec-ca- ta

50
lis pec- ca-
mun- di,
mi- se- re-
ta mun-
55
di, mi- se- re- re
mi- se- re-
60
no-
re no-
re no-
65
bis.
bis.
bis.

C
70
A - gnus de - i qui
A - gnus de - i qui
A - gnus
A - gnus de - i qui
75
tol - lis pec - ca -
tol - lis pe - ca -
de - i qui tol - lis pec -
tol - lis pec - ca - ta
80
ta mun - di, do -
ta mun - di, do - na
ca - ta mun - di, do - na no -
mun - di, do - na no -
85
90
na no - bis pa - cem.
no - bis pa - cem.
bis pa - se - cem.
bis pa - cem.

19 GUILLAUME DU FAY *Missa L'homme armé:* Agnus Dei

mun - di, mi - - se -
- - - - - - - - - - - - - - - - - - di,
mun - di, pec - ca - - - ta mun - di,
- - - - - - - - - - - - ta mun - - - - - - - - - - - -
re - - - - - - - - - - - - re no - - - - - - -
mi - se - re - - - - - - - - - - - - re, mi - se - re - re no - -
mi - se - - re - - re, mi - se - re - - re
di, mi - se - re - - - - - re
- bis.
- bis.
no - - bis, no - bis, mi - se - re - re no - - bis.
no - - - - - - - - - - - - - - - - - - bis.
B
A - - - - gnus de - - - - - - i
Contra
A - - - - - - gnus de - - - - - - - i qui
Contra bassus

50
qui tol - - - - - - - - - - - - - - -
tol - - - - - - - - - - lis pec -
55
lis pec - ca - - - ta mun - - - - - - - - - - di,
- - - - ca - - ta mun - - - - - di,
60
mi - se - re - - -
mi se - re - - - re, mi se - re - - - - - - - re, mi - se - re -
mi - se - re - re, mi - se - re - - - - - - - - - - - - - - - re,
65
- - - - - - - - re no - - - - - - - - - bis, - mi - se -
re, mi - se - re - re no - - - - - - bis,
mi - se - re - re no - - - - - - - - - - - -
70
re - re no - - - - - - - - - - - - - - - - bis.
mi - se - re - re no - - - - - - - - - - - bis.
- bis.

(1) *Canon:* Cancer eat plenus sed redeat medius.

105
di, pec_ca _ ta mun_
110
115
di, do_
di, do
di, do_ na nobis, do_
di, do_
120
na no_
na no_
na no_ bis, do_na no_ bis, do_na no bis pa_
na no_
125
130
bis pa_ cem.
bis pa cem.
cem, do_na no_ bis pa_ cem.
bis pa_ cem.

20 GILLES BINCHOIS *Magnificat tercii toni*

24
gna qui po - tens est et San -
gna qui po - tens est et San -
gna qui po - tens est et San -
30
ctam no - men e - - - - - jus. Fe - cit po - ten - - ti -
ctam no - men e - - - - - jus. Fe - cit po - ten - - ti -
ctam no - men e - - - - - jus. Fe - cit po - ten - ti -
37
am in bra - chi - o su - - o,
am in bra - chi - o su - - o,
am in bra - chi - o su - - o,
44
di - sper - sit su - per - - bos men - te cor - dis su -
di - sper - sit su - per - bos men - te cor - dis su -
di - sper - sit su - per - bos men - te cor - dis su -

51
- - i. E - su - - ri - en - - tes im - ple -
- - i. E - su - - ri - en - - tes im - ple -
- - i. E - su - - ri - en - - tes im - ple -
58
- vit bo - - - - - nis; et di - vi - tes
- vit bo - - - - - nis; et di - vi - tes
- vit bo - - - - - nis; et di - vi - tes
66
di - mi - sit in - a - - - - - nes. Si - cut lo -
di - mi - sit in - a - - - - - nes. Si - cut lo -
di - mi - sit in - a - - - - - nes. Si - cut lo -
73
cu - tus est ad Pa - - tres no - stros;
cu - tus est ad Pa - - tres no - stros;
cu - tus est ad Pa - - tres no - stros;

79
A - bra - - ham et se - mi - ni e - jus in se - cu -
A - bra - - ham et se - mi - ni e - jus in se - cu -
A - bra - - ham et se - mi - ni e - jus in se -
85
- - - - la. Si - cut e - rat in prin - ci - pi -
- - - - la. Si - cut e - rat in prin - ci - pi -
cu - - - la. Si - cut e - rat in prin - ci - pi -
91
o, et nunc et sem - per, et in
o, et nunc et sem - per, et in
o, et nunc et sem - per, et in
97
se - cu - la se - cu - lo - rum. A - - - - men.
se - cu - la se - cu - lo - rum. A - - - - men.
se - cu - la se - cu - lo - rum. A - - - - men.

21 ANTOINE BUSNOYS *Missa L'homme armé:* Agnus Dei

Antoine Busnoys, *Collected Works*. Parts 2 and 3: The Latin Texted Works. Ed. Taruskin. In Masters and Monuments of the Renaissance 5/2–3 (New York: The Broude Trust, 1990), pp. 41–48. Used by permission.

13
-i, qui
- -i, qui tol-
Qui tol- lis
Qui tol- lis, *tol-*
17
tol-
- -lis pec- ca-
pec- ca- ta mun-
-lis pec- ca- ta, pec- ca- ta
21
-lis pec- ca- ta mun-
-ta mun- *di,*
- *di, mun-* di:
mun- di:

25
- -di: mi- se- re-
mun- di, mun- di:
mi- se- re-
mi- se- re- re,
29
- -re no-
mi- se- re- re, mi- se-
- -re, mi-
mi- se- re- re
33
-bis, no- -bis.
re- re no- -bis.
- se- re- -re no- -bis.
no- bis.

Bass
A- gnus De-
A- gnus De-
[Agnus II tacet]
-i,
-i, qui tol-
Qui tol-

15
pec- ca- ta mun-
- -lis:
- -lis pec- ca- ta mun-
19
-
-
22
-di: mi- se- re- re no-
mi- se- re-
- -di: mi- se- re- re
25
- -bis.
-re no- -bis.
no- bis.

Contratenor
Tenor
Tenor
Canon ut supra
A- gnus De- i,
A- gnus, A- gnus, A- gnus, A-
A- gnus De- i,
qui tol- lis pec-
qui tol-
i, qui tol- lis, qui
qui tol- lis,
-ca- ta mun- di,

10
- lis pec- ca-
tol-
tol- lis pec- ca- ta
qui tol- lis pec-
12
- ta mun- di, mun-
- lis pec- ca- ta mun- di:
mun- di, mun- di, mun- di, mun- di:
- ca- ta
15
- di: do- na no-
do- na no- bis,
do- na no- bis,
mun- di: do- na

17
20)
- bis pa- cem, pa- cem.
no- bis pa- cem, pa- cem.
no- bis pa- cem, pa- cem.
no- bis pa- cem.

22 ROBERT MORTON *Il sera pour vous / L'ome armé*

Tenor
Contra
1. 4. 7. Il se - ra pour vous con - - ba - tu, Le doub - té turcq, Mai - stre Sy - mon.
3. Son or - gueil te - nons a - - ba - tu, S'il chiet en voz mains le fe - lon.
5. En peu de heu - re l'a - rés ba - tu, Au plai - sir dieu, puis di - ra on:
2. 8. Cer - tai - ne - ment,
6. Vi - ve Sy - mon -,
L'o - me, l'o - me, l'o - me ar - mé, l'o - me ar - mé, l'o - me ar - mé doibt on doub - ter, et l'o - me ar - mé. On a fait par tout cri -
L'o - me, l'o - me, l'o - me ar - mé, l'o - me ar - mé doibt on doub - ter, l'o - me ar - mé, A l'as - sault, et a l'as - sault,
3
6

Robert Morton, *The Collected Works*. Ed. Atlas. In Masters and Monuments of the Renaissance 2 (New York, Broude Bros., 1981), pp. 7–8. Used by permission.

9
cer- tai- ne- ment, cer- tai- ne- ment ce se- ra
vi- ve Sy- mon-, vi- ve Sy- mon- et le bre-
- er: A l'as- sault, d'un hau- bre- gon de
Que chas- cun se vie- gne‿ar- mer,
12
mon, Et de crocq de ach- e‿a- ba-
- ton, Que sur le turcq s'est en- ba-
fer. L'o- me, l'o- me, l'o- me‿ar- mé,
1)
A l'as- sault, a l'as- sault. L'o- me, l'o- me, l'o- me‿ar- mé, l'o- me‿ar-
15
- tu, *de ach- e‿a- ba- tu.*
- tu, *le turcq s'est en- ba- tu.*
l'o- me‿ar- mé, l'o- me‿ar- mé doibt on doub- ter.
- mé, l'o- me‿ar- mé doibt on doub- ter.

23 ANTOINE BUSNOYS *In hydraulis*

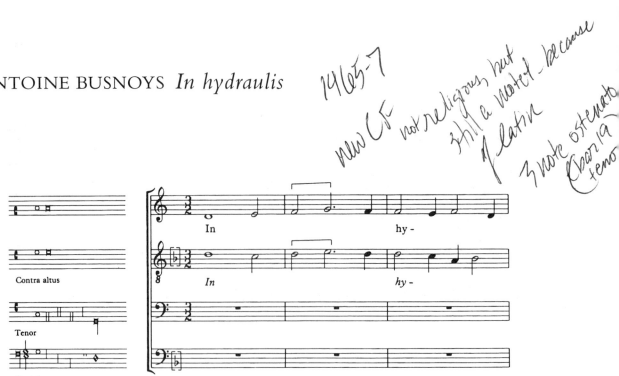

Antoine Busnoys, *Collected Works*. Parts 2 and 3: The Latin Texted Works. Ed. Taruskin. In Masters and Monuments of the Renaissance 5/2–3 (New York: The Broude Trust, 1990), pp. 151–56. Used by permission.

12
me -
- mi- ran- te me-
- mi- ran- te me-
16
- los phton- gi- ta-
- los phton- gi- ta- tes Mal-
[O-
[RE
- los phton- gi- ta- tes
20
- tes Mal- le- o-
- le- o-
- KE- GHEM(?)] etc.
UT RE
Mal- le- o-

24
- rum per- cus-
- -rum per-
LA SOL
- rum per- cus-
28
-sa ae- quo- ra
-cus- sa ae- quo- ra
LA RE
-sa ae- quo- ra
32
Per pon- de- rum in- ae-
Per pon- de- rum in-
UT RE
Per pon- de- rum in- ae-

musica ficta
ligature
36
- qua - li - ta -
- ae - qua - li - ta -
RE UT
- quae - li - ta - tes Ad -
40
-tes Ad - in - ve - nit,
-tes Ad - in - ve - nit, ad - in - ve -
RE LA
- in - ve - nit, ad - in - ve - nit
44
mu - sae qui - di -
- nit mu - sae qui - di -
SOL LA
mu - sae qui -

48
-ta- tes. E-
-ta- tes. E- pi-
RE UT
-di- ta- tes. E-
52
-pi- tri- tum ac he- mi- o- li-
-tri- tum ac he- mi- o- li- am,
RE
-pi- tri- tum ac he- mi- o- li- am, he-
56
-am, he- mi- o- li- am, ac he- mi- o- li- am, ac he- mi- o- li-
-mi- o- li- am, ac he- mi- o- li- am, ac he- mi- o- li- am, E-

59
-am, E-pog-do- i et du-plam per-du- cunt
E- pog- do- i et du- plam
C
RE UT
-pog-do- i et- du- plam per- du- cunt
63
Nam tes- sa- ron pen- te con-
per- du- cunt Nam tes- sa-
RE LA SOL LA
Nam tes- sa- ron pen- te con-
68
- cor- di- am Nec
- ron pen- te con- cor- di-
RE UT
-cor- di- am Nec

71
non phton - gum et pa - son
- am Nec non phton - gum
RE RE
non phton - gum
74
ad - du - cunt, ad - du -
et pa -
UT RE
et pa - son ad -
77
- cunt, ad - du - cunt Mo - no - cor -
- son ad - du - cunt Mo - no - cor - di
LA SOL LA
- du - cunt Mo - no - cor - di dum ge - nus

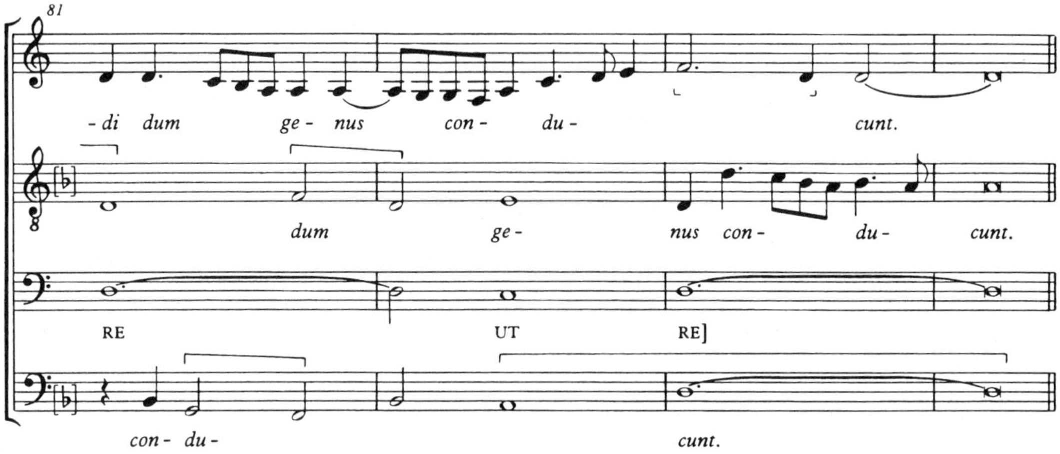
81
-di dum ge- nus con- du- cunt.
dum ge- nus con- du- cunt.
RE UT RE]
con- du- cunt.

24 JOHANNES OCKEGHEM *Missa Prolationum:* Kyrie and Sanctus

Christe eleison

pausans ascendit per unum

9
ste e - lei - son. Chri - ste e - lei - son.
ste e - lei - son. Chri - ste e - lei - son.
12
Chri - ste e - lei - son.
Chri - ste e - lei - son.
15
Chri - ste e - lei - son. Chri - ste e - lei -
Chri - ste e - lei - son. Chri - ste e - lei -

17
son. Chri - ste e - lei - son.
son. Chri - ste e- lei - son.
20
Chri - ste e - lei - son. Chri - ste e - lei -
Chri - ste e - lei - son. Chri - ste e - lei -
22
son. Chri - ste e - lei - son.
son. Chri - ste e - lei - son.

Kyrie eleison II

Sanctus

fuga pausarum ascendendo per sextam

Pleni

fuga post unum ○ tempus descendendo per septimam

glo - ri - a tu - a.
ter - ra glo - ri - a tu - a.
Osanna
O - san - na in ex - cel - sis.
O - san - na
O - san - na in ex - cel - sis.
O - san - na in
O - san - na in ex - cel - sis. O-
in ex - cel - sis. O - san - na in ex - cel -
O - san - na in ex - cel - sis. O - san -
ex - cel - sis. O - san -
san - na in ex - cel - sis.
sis. O - san - na in ex - cel - sis.
na in ex - cel - sis.
na in ex - cel - sis. O - san - na in ex - cel - sis.

Benedictus

Previous 𝅗𝅥 = 𝅗𝅥.

10
di - ctus qui ve -
ne - di - ctus qui ve -
13
in no - mi - ne Do -
nit
in no - mi - ne Do -
nit
17

Osanna *ut supra*

25a JOHANNES OCKEGHEM *Fors seulement*

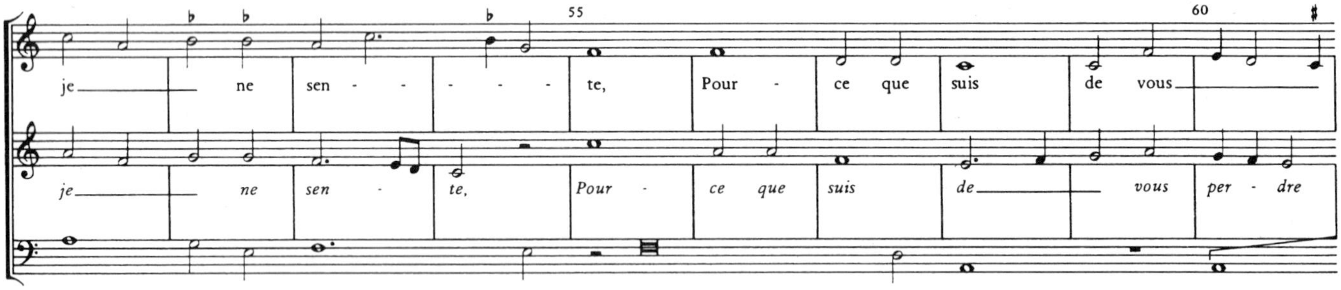

2. Vostre rigueur tellement m'y queurt seure
Qu'en ce parti il fault que je m'asseure,
Dont je n'ay bien qui en riens me contente
Fors seulement l'actente . . .

4. Mon desconfort toute seule je pleure,
En maudisant sur ma foy a toute heure
Ma leauté qui tant m'a fait dolente.
Las, que je suis de vivre mal contente
Quant de par vous n'ay riens qui me demeure
Fors seulement l'actente . . .

25b JOHANNES OCKEGHEM *Missa Fors seulement:* Kyrie

23
son.
ri - e e - lei - son.
son, e - lei - son.
son, Ky - ri - e e - lei - son.
Ky - ri - e e - lei - son.
30
Chri - ste e - lei -
Chri - ste e -
Chri - ste e - lei -
Chri - ste, Chri - ste e - lei -
Chri - ste e - lei - son,
37
son, e - lei - son, Chri - ste e -
lei - son, e -
son, Chri - ste e - lei - son.
son, Chri - ste e - lei -
e - lei - son, e - lei -

44
-lei - - - - - - - - son.
- - lei - - - son.
Ky - - - ri - - e e - lei - - -
- - - - - - - - - - - - - son. Ky - - ri - - e e - - lei -
- - - - - - - - - - - - - - - son. Ky - ri - e e - - - lei - - -
51
Ky - ri - - - e e - lei - - - - - - - -
Ky - - - - - ri - e e - lei - - - - - - -
- - - - - - - - - - - - - - son, Ky - - - - - - - - - - - -
- - - - - - - - - - son, e - lei - - - son,
- - - son, Ky - - - - - - - - - rie,
57
- - - - - son, e - - lei - - - - - - - - - - - - - - - -
- - - - son, Ky - - - ri - - e e - - -
- - ri - e e - lei - - - - - - - - - - - - - - - - -
Ky - ri - e e - - - lei - - - - - - - son,
Ky - - - - ri - e e - lei - - - - - - - - - - - - -

64
(♯)
son, Ky - ri - e e - lei -
lei - son, Ky - ri - e e - lei -
son, e - lei -
Ky - ri - e e - lei -
son, Ky - ri -
70
son.
son.
son.
son.
e e - lei - son.

26 JOHANNES REGIS *Clangat plebs flores*

Cui cle _ ro col _
Cui cle _ ro col _
tat abs _ que mo _ _ ra.
res de _ pu _ tat abs _ que mo _ ra.
_ lo con _ ce _ dan car _ mi _ na ca _ ro cum
_ lo con _ ce _ dan car _ mi _ na ca _ ro cum
Cum can _
Cum
can _ tu cle _ ro con _ gru _ e cun _ cta ca _ ro ut vi _ ven _ tem post pe _
can _ tu cle _ ro con _ gru _ e cun _ cta ca _ ro ut vi _ ven _ tem
Sic _ ut li _
tu cle _ ro con _ gru _ e cun _ cta cla _ ro
can tu cle _

20
tat or - bem mu - ne_re Chi_
post pe - tat or - bem mu - ne - re Chri - sti,
_li - um
mu - ne - re Chri_
_ro
23
sti nos ra_di_en - tem fe - li_ci_ta - tem scan_de_re cæ_
(Chri - sti)
sti nos ra_di_en - tem fe - li_ci_ta - tem scan_de_re cæ_
26
li, sed qui_a ter_ri_bi_li vi_ci_o - rum mol - le re - fer_ri pos_su_mus
Sed qui - a ter - ri - bi_li vi_ci_o - rum mol - le re_fer_ri pos_su_mus hanc
li

29
hanc di - gne can_ti_ca por_ri - ge - re e_xi_ge_re cun_ctis ut
di - gne can - ti_ca por_ri - ge_re
in_
hinc ve_ni_am la_psis_pro_
hinc ve - ni_am la - psis pro
32
ro_gi_ta - tu tu - o com_pla_ce_ant Do_
ut ro - gi - ta - tu com_pla - ce_ant
ter spi_ _nas,
su - is com - pla - ce - ant Do_
su_is e_xi - ge - re cun_ctis com - pla - ce_ant
35
_mi - no. Car - mi_na ca - den - tem ti_
Do - mi - no. Car - mi - na ca - den - tem ti - bi
(spinas.) sic
_mi - no. Car - mi - na
Do - mi - no. Car - mi_na ca_

40
bi flo_ri _da pro _spi _ ce vir - go, ma _ xi _ me de _ flen_te me
flo _ ri _ da pro_spi_ce vir - go, ma _ xi _ me de _ flen_te me
a _ mi _ ca me_a
ca_den _ tem ri _ bi flo _ ri _ da
_ den_ tem ti _ bi flo _ ri _ da
46
quo_que pro vi_ci _ o me di _ gna_ _re tu_
quo_que pro vi _ ci _ o me di _ gna_
(me _ a) in_
pro _ spi _ ce vir _ go ma _ xi_me de_
pro _ spi _ ce vir _ go ma _ xi _ me
52
os bo_ _stes cun _ ctos
re tu _ os bo - stes cun_ctos su _ per_a
ter fi_
flen _ te me quo _ que pro vi _ ci _ o
de _ flen _ te me quo _ que pro vi _ ci _ o

57
su_per_a - re
et te lau_da_re va_
re et te lau - da_re va_
li - as
me di_gna - re
me di_gna - re
63
_le_am
le - am
tu_os bo - stes cun_ctos
tu - os bo - stes cun_ctos
68
ge - ni_trix - que be_a_
ge - ni_trix - que be - a
su - per - a - re.
su_per_a re.

73
_re cor_po_re di_vi_
_re cor_po_re di - vi_
79
na di - re - cto tra - mi - te do_
na di - re - cto tra - mi - te do_
84
_na Hac ma_la ter_ge ma - lis
_na Hac ma_la ter_ge ma_
sic - ut li - li_um
Sic - ut li - li

90
(#) (#) stel - la Ma - ri - a ma - ris, stel -
- lis stel - la Ma - ri - a ma - ris
in - ter spi - nas sic
um in - ter spi - nas
96
li - fe - ri
stel - li -
a - mi - ca me - a
sic a - mi - ca me -
101
re - gi - na mi - cans quo - que
- fe - ri re - gi - na mi - cans
in - ter fi - li - as (in
- a in - ter fi - li - as

106
lu men or - ti pel - li fe - ri
quo - que lu - men or - ti pel - li-
-ter fi - li -as) (Sic a - mi - ca
(Sic a - mi - ca me - a in-
Hac ma-
112
pœ - (nas gens, pœ) - nas gens cun-
-fe - ri pœ - nas gens cunc-
me - a, a - mi - ca me - a, a - mi - ca me - a in - ter
ter fi - li - as)
(b)
-la ter - ge ma-
118
-cta det. A - men.
-cta det. A - men.
fi- -li - as) A - men.
A - men.
-lis. A men.

27 ANTOINE BUSNOYS *Je ne puis vivre*

Quant a moi, je me meurs bon cours,
Vellant les nuytz, faisant cent tours,
En criant fort:
"Vengeance!" a Dieu, car a grant tort
Je noye en plours
Lorsqu'au besoing me fault secours—
Et Pitié dort.

Je ne . . . la mort.

 Perkins and Garey, eds., *The Mellon Chansonnier* (New Haven, CT: Yale University Press, 1979), pp. 65–67.

28 JOHANNES OCKEGHEM *S'elle m'amera / Petite camusette*

Perkins and Garey, eds., *The Mellon Chansonnier* (New Haven, CT: Yale University Press, 1979), p. 45. 141

29 HAYNE VAN GHIZEGHEM *De tous biens plaine*

1. 4. 7. De tous biens plai - ne est ma mais - tres - se, Chas - cun luy doibt tri - but d'hon - neur;
3. En la voi - ant j'ay tel lé - es - se Que c'est pa - ra - dis en mon cueur.
5. Je n'ay cu - re d'aul - tre rich - es - se Si non d'es - tre son ser - vi - teur,
Tenor
De tous biens
Contra
De tous biens
5
10
15
20
25

[𝄐]
30
2. 8. Car as - - sou - vye est
6. Et pour - ce qu'il n'est
35
40
en va - - leur
chois meil - - leur
45
Au - tant que ja - - mais fut
En mon mot por - - te - ray sans
50
dé - es -
ces -
55
60
- se.
- se

30 JOHN BEDYNGHAM OR WALTER FRYE *So ys emprentid*

25
that lor - de al - le wot tak y to wit - - - nes -
30
- se that walky, slep - ey, or wat thing y
35
do, in we - le, in wo, in jo - ye ore heu -
40
e - nes - se, myn hert ys with
45
yow, go wey that ye go.

31 ANONYMOUS *Mein herz in steten trewen*

Tenor
Contra
Mein herz in ste - ten tre - - wen in
die mir mein freud tut me - ren van
5
1.(2.)
hoff - nung zu dir was;
tag je lenger je paß.
ir lib hat mich umb -
10
- fan - gen, welch end ich mich hin - ker; nach
15
ir stet mein ver - lan - gen, mein un - mut wer ver -
- gan - gen, het mich die zart ge - wert.

 Reinhard Strohm, *The Rise of European Music, 1380–1500* (Cambridge: Cambridge University Press, 1994), pp. 498–99. Reprinted with the permission of Cambridge University Press.

32 JOAN CORNAGO *¿Qu'es mi vida preguntays?*

[Discantus]
Tenor
Contratenor
5
[¿Qu'es mi vi- da,] pre- gun-
¿Pa- ra que me, pre- gun-
[¿Qu'es mi vida,] preguntays?
[¿Qu'es mi vida,] preguntays?
10
- tays? Non vos la quie- ro ne- gar, Bien a- mar e la- men-
- tays? La pe- na que he de pas- sar, Pues a- mar e la- men-
15
- tar, [bien a- mar e la- men- tar] Es la vi-
- tar, [pues a- mar e la- men- tar]

Rebecca L. Gerber, ed., *Johannes Cornago: Complete Works,* Recent Researches in the Music of the Middle Ages and Early Renaissance, vol. 15 (Madison, WI: A-R Editions, Inc., 1984), pp. xxv–xvi (text), 51–53 (music).

Fine
- - da que me days.
¿Quien vos pu- die- ra ser- - -
¿Mi tra- ba- xa- do vi- - -
- vir Tam- bien co- mo [yo]he ser- vi- do, [ser- -
- vir Quien pu- die- ra haver so- fri- do, [so- -
D.C. al Fine
- vi- - - - do?]
- fri- - - - - do?]

33 SERAFINO DALL'AQUILA *Sufferir son disposto*

Reposo me sarria esser contento,
contento de l'Amor che porto ascuso.

Ascuso focho nel [mio] peto sento,
sento che me consuma el cor doglioso.

Doglioso vivo et del mio mal consento,
consento de morir, o gloriuso.

Allan Atlas, *Music at the Aragonese Court of Naples* (Cambridge: Cambridge University Press, 1985), p. 223. Reprinted with the permission of Cambridge University Press.

34a ROBERT MORTON *Le souvenir*

1. 4. 7. Le sou - ve - nir de vous me tu -
3. Quant vous es - tes hor de ma vu -
5. Seu - le de -meu - re des - pour -ve - u -
Le souvenir de vous
Tenor
Le souvenir de vous
Contra
4
- e, Mon seul bien, mon seul bien, quant je ne vous
- e, Je me plains, je me plains et dis a par
- e, D'a - me nul, d'a - me nul con - fort ne re -
7
voy.
moy,
çoy.
2. 8. Car je vous ju - re,
6. Et si seuf - fre,

 Robert Morton, *The Collected Works*. Ed. Atlas. In Masters and Monuments of the Renaissance 2 (New York: Broude Bros., 1981), pp. 15–17.

car je vous ju-   re sur   ma foy,   sur
et si seuf-   fre sans   fai - re ef -froy,   sans

        ma foy,   Sans vous ma li - es -   se, ma li -
fai - re ef - froy,   Jus - ques a vos-   tre,   a   vos -

-        es -   se est per -   du -   e.
-        tre   re - ve -   nu -   e.

34b ROBERT MORTON *Le souvenir,* instrumental arrangement

 Robert Morton, *The Collected Works.* Ed. Atlas. In Masters and Monuments of the Renaissance 2 (New York: Broude Bros., 1981), pp. 20–22.

10
12
14
tr
16
18
3
3
3
3

35 JOHANNES MARTINI *La martinella*

Edward G. Evans, Jr., ed., *Johannes Martini: Secular Pieces,* Recent Researches in the Music of the Middle Ages and Early Renaissance, vol. 1 (Madison, WI: A-R Editions, Inc., 1975), pp. 47–49.

[Secunda pars]

36 GUGLIELMO EBREO *Falla con misuras*

Allan Atlas, *Music at the Aragonese Court of Naples* (Cambridge: Cambridge University Press, 1985), pp. 230–31. Reprinted with the permission of Cambridge University Press.

30
35
40
3
45

37 JOSQUIN DESPREZ *Ave Maria . . . virgo serena*

Edited by Alejandro Enrique Planchart. Used by permission.

13
Vir - go se - re - na, se - re - na. A - ve, cu -
re - - - - - na, se - re - na. A - ve, cu -
Vir - go se - re - - - - na.
cum, Vir - - go se - re - na.
17
ius con-ce - pti - o sol -
ius con-ce - pti - o, con - ce - pti - o sol -
A - ve, cu - ius con-ce - pti - o sol -
A - ve, cu - ius con-ce - pti - o sol -
21
lem-ni ple - na gau - di - o, Cae - le - sti - a, ter - re - stri - a no -
lem-ni ple - na gau-di-o, Cae-le-sti - a, ter - re-stri-a no -
lem-ni ple - na gau - di - o, Cae-le - sti - a, ter - re - stri - a no - va
lem-ni ple - na gau - di - o, Cae-le - sti - a, ter-re - stri - a no-

25
va re - plet lae - - ti - ti - a. A - ve, cu-ius na -
va re-plet lae-ti - - ti - a. A - ve, cu-ius
re - plet lae - - ti - - ti - a.
va re - plet lae - ti - ti - a.

25
va re - plet lae - - ti - ti - a. A - ve, cu-ius na -
va re-plet lae-ti - - ti - a. A - ve, cu-ius
re - plet lae - - ti - - ti - a.
va re - plet lae - ti - ti - a.

29
ti - vi-tas, na-ti - vi - tas Ut
na - ti - vi-tas, na-ti-vi-tas
No - stra fu - it sol-lem - ni - tas, sol-lem - ni -
No-stra fu-it sol-lem - ni-tas, sol-lem-ni -

33
lu - ci - fer, lux o - ri - ens, Ve - rum so -
Ut lu - ci - fer, lux o - ri - ens, Ve - rum so - lem
tas: Ut lu - ci - fer, lux o - ri - ens, Ve - rum so -
tas: Ut lu - ci - fer, lux o - ri -

37
lem, ve - rum so - lem prae - ve - ni - ens. A - ve, pi - a hu - mi - li -
prae - ve - ni - ens. A - ve, pi - a hu - mi - li -
lem prae - ve - ni - ens, prae - ve - ni - ens.
ens, Ve - rum so - lem prae - ve - ni - ens.

41
tas, Cu - ius an - nun - ti - a - ti - o
tas, Cu - ius an - nun - ti - a - ti - o
Si - ne vi - ro fe - cun - di - tas, No -
Si - ne vi - ro fe - cun - di - tas, No -

45
A - ve, ve - ra vir - gi - ni -
A - ve, ve - ra vir - gi - ni -
stra fu - it sal - va - - ti - o. A - ve, ve - ra vir - gi -
stra fu - it sal - va - - ti - - o. A - ve, ve - ra vir - gi - ni -
49
tas, Im - ma - cu - la - ta ca - sti - tas, Cu - ius pu - ri - fi - ca - ti -
tas, Im - ma - cu - la - ta ca - sti - tas, Cu - ius pu - ri - fi - ca - ti -
ni - tas, Im - ma - cu - la - ta ca - sti - tas, Cu - ius pu - ri - fi - ca -
tas, Im - ma - cu - la - ta ca - sti - tas, Cu - ius pu - ri - fi - ca - ti -
53
o No - stra fu - it pur - ga - ti - o. A - ve, prae -
o No - stra fu - it pur - ga - ti - o. A - ve, prae -
ti - o No - stra fu - it pur - ga - ti - o.
o No - stra fu - it pur - ga - ti - o.

57
cla - - ra om - ni - bus, An - ge - li -
cla - ra om - ni - bus, An - ge - li -
A - ve, prae - cla - - ra om - ni - bus,
A - ve, prae - cla - ra om - - - ni - bus,
61
cis vir - tu - ti - bus, cu - ius fu -
cis vir - tu - ti - bus, cu - ius fu -
An - ge - li - cis vir - tu - ti - bus,
An - ge - li - cis vir - tu - - ti - bus,
65
it as - sum - pti - o no - stra glo - ri - fi -
it as - sum - pti - - o no - stra, no -
cu - ius fu - it as - sum - pti - o
cu - ius fu - it as - sum - pti - o

69
ca - ti - o.
- stra glo - - ri - fi - ca - - ti - o.
no - stra glo - ri - - fi - ca - ti - - o.
no - stra glo - - ri - fi - ca - ti - o.
73
O Ma - ter De - - - i, me - men - to
O Ma - ter De - - - i, me - men - to
O Ma - ter De - - - i, me - men - to
O Ma - ter De - - - i, me - men - to
76
me - - i. A - - men.
me - - i. A - - men.
me - - i. A - - men.
me - - i. A - - men.

38 HEINRICH ISAAC *Quis dabit capiti meo aquam?*

23
no - - - - - cte fle - - - - - - - - - - - am, ut lu - ce
- - - - - bit, ut lu - - - - ce fle - - - - - - - - -
- am, ut lu - - - - ce fle - - - - - - -
31
fle - am? Sic tur - tur vi - du - us so - - - - - let, sic cy - gnus
- - - am? Sic tur - tur vi - du - us so - - - - - - - - let, sic cy - gnus
Sic tur - tur vi - du - us so - - - - - let, sic cy - gnus
- am? Sic tur - tur vi - du - us so - - - - let, sic cy - gnus
40
mo - ri - ens so - - - - - - - - - - let, sic lu - sci - ni -
mo - ri - ens so - - - - - - - - - - - - - - let, sic lu - sci - ni -
mo - ri - ens so - - - - - - - - - - let.
mo - ri - ens so - - - - - - - - - - - - - - let, sic lu - sci - ni -
49
- a con - que - - - - - ri, con - que - - - - - - - - - ri. Heu
- a con - - - - - - - - - que - ri, Heu mi -
Heu mi - ser, o
- a con - que - - - - - ri. Heu mi - ser, o

56
mi - - - - - - - - - - ser, o do - - - lor, do - - -
- - - ser, mi - ser, o do - - - - - - lor, do - - - - - -
do - - - - lor, do - - - lor!
do - - - - lor, do - - - - - - - - lor!
Secunda pars.
63
- - - - - lor! Lau - rus im - pe - te ful - - - - - - - - - - - mi -
lor! Lau - rus, lau - rus im - pe - te ful - mi -
Tenor Laurus tacet.
Et re - qui - e - sca - mus in pa - ce,
71
nis il - la il - la ia - - - - cet su - - - - - - - - bi -
nis il - la il - la ia - - - - - - - - - - - - cet su - bi -
et re - qui - e - sca - mus in pa - ce,
78
to, lau - - - - - - - - - rus
to, lau - - - - rus, lau - - - - rus o - mni - um ce - le -
et re - qui - e - sca - mus in pa - ce, et re - qui -

86
o - mni- um ce - - - - - - - - - le - - - bris mu -
bris mu - sa - rum cho - - - - - - - - - - - ris, nym - - - - -
e - sca- mus in pa - ce, et re - qui -
92
sa - rum cho - - - - - - ris, nym - pha - - - - - - rum cho -
- - - - - - - - pha - rum cho - - - - - - - - ris, nym - pha -
e - sca - mus in pa - ce, et re - qui -
Tertia pars.
98
- - - - - - - - - - - - - - - - - ris. Sub cu - ius pa - tu - la
rum cho - - - - - - - ris. Sub cu - ius pa - tu - la
Sub cu - ius pa -
e - sca- mus in pa - - - ce. Sub cu - ius pa - tu - la
86
o - mni- um ce - - - - - - - - - le - - - bris mu -
bris mu - sa - rum cho - - - - - - - - - - - ris, nym - - - - -
e - sca- mus in pa - ce, et re - qui -

114
blan - - - - - - - - - di - us in - so - nat et vox blan - -
blan - di - us in - so - nat et vox blan - - - -
-ra blan - - - di - - - us so - nat
blan - - - - - - - - - di - us et vox blan - -
122
- - - - - - - - - - - - - - - di - us nunc mu - ta om - - - - - - - -
- - - - - di - us in - - - - - so - nat nunc mu - - - - -
nunc mu - ta om - - - - - - ni -
di - us in - so - - - nat,
128
-ni - - - a, om - ni - a, nunc sur - da om - - - - - - - ni -
- - - - - ta om - ni - a, om - ni - a, nunc sur - - - - - - da
-a, nunc sur - da om - - - - - - ni -
in - - - - so - - - - nat, nunc sur - da om - - - - - - - ni -
135
-a.
om - - - - - - - - - - - - - - - - - - ni - a.
-a.
-a, nunc mu - - - - - - ta om - ni - a.

39 JOSQUIN DESPREZ OR PIERRE DE LA RUE *Absalon, fili mi*

Josquin Desprez, *Werken*. Supplement. Ed. Smijers et al. (Amsterdam: Vereniging voor Nederlandse Muziekgeschiedenis, 1969), pp. 22–25.

20
sa - lon, fi - li mi, Ab - sa - lon,
sa - lon, Ab - sa - lon, fi -
Ab - sa - lon, fi - - - - li mi, fi - li mi,
sa - lon, fi - li mi,
25
fi - li mi,
li mi,
Ab - sa - lon,
fi - li mi, Ab - - - -
30
fi - li mi, Ab -
fi - li mi,
fi - li mi, Ab - sa - lon, fi - li mi, fi - li mi,
- - sa - lon, Ab - - sa - lon, Ab -
35
- - sa - lon, Ab - - sa - lon, quis det
Ab - sa - lon,
Ab - - -
- - sa - lon, fi - li mi, quis

ut mo - - ri - ar pro te,
quis det ut mo - ri - ar pro te,
- sa - lon, fi - li mi. quis det ut mo - -
det ut mo - ri - ar pro te, ut mo - ri - ar
fi - li mi, Ab - sa - lon?
ut mo - ri - ar pro te, fi - li mi, Ab - sa - lon?
- - ri - ar pro te, fi - li mi Ab - - sa - lon?
pro te, fi - li mi, Ab - sa - lon?
Non vi - vam ul - - tra,
Non vi - - vam ul - - tra,
Non vi - - - - vam, vi - - - -
Non vi - vam ul - - - -
non vi - vam ul - - tra, sed de - scen-
non vi - vam ul - - tra, sed
vam ul - - tra, sed de - - scen - -
tra, ul - - - -tra, sed de -

65
dam in in- fer- num plo-
dé- scen- dam in in- fer- num plo-
dam in in- fer- num plo-
scen- dam in in- fer- num plo- rans,
70
rans, non vi- vam ul- tra, non
rans, non vi- vam ul- tra, non
rans, non vi- vam
(♭) non vi- vam ul- tra,
75
vi- vam ul- tra, sed de- scen- dam
vi- vam ul- tra, sed de- scen-
ul- tra, sed de- scen- dam in
ul- tra, sed de- scen-
80
85
in in- fer- num plo- rans.
dam in in- fer- num plo- rans.
in- fer num plo- rans.
dam in in- fer- num plo- rans.

40 JOSQUIN DESPREZ *Miserere mei, Deus*

The Medici Codex of 1518 (Chicago: University of Chicago Press, 1968).

20
- am tu - - - - am
- se - ri - cor - di - am tu - am
Mi - se - re - re me - i de -
mi - - se - re - re me - i de -
mi - se - re - re me - i de -
25
et se - cun -
et se - cun - - dum mul - ti -
- us
- us mi - se - re - re
- us
30
- dum mul - ti - tu - di - nem mi - se - ra - ti - o - num tu -
- tu - - di - nem mi - se - ra - - ti - o - num tu -

35
- - a - - - - rum de - le de - le in -
- a - - rum de - le in - i - qui - ta -
40
- i - qui - ta - tem me - - - am Mi - - se - re - re me - i de -
- tem me - - - - am mi - se - re - re me -
Mi - se - re - re me - i
mi - se - re - re me - i
mi - se - re - re me - i
45
- - us am - pli - us la - ua me ab
- i de - - us am - pli - us la - ua me ab
de - - us
de - - us am - pli - us la - ua me ab
de - - us am - pli - us la - ua me ab

50
in - i - qui - ta - te me - - a
in - i - qui - ta - te me - a et a pec - ca - to me - o
in - i - qui - ta - te me - a et a pec - ca - to me - -
in - i - qui - ta - te me - a et a pec - ca -
55
et a pec - ca - to me - o mun - da me
mun - - da me
mi - se -
- - o mun - - da me mun - - da me
- to me - o mun - da me
60
quo - ni - am in -
mi - se - re - re me - i de - - us
-re - re me - i de - - us
mi - se - re - re me - i de - - us quo - ni -
mi - se - re - re me - i de - us

65
-i - qui - ta - - - - tem___ me - - - am e - go co -
8 - am in - i - qui - ta - tem_____ me - am e - go co - gno - sco
e - go co -
70
-gno - - -sco et pec - ca - tum me - um con - tra_ me_ est sem - -
Et pec - ca - tum me - - um con - tra me est sem -
E - go co - gno - sco
-Gno - - - sco
75
-per mi - - se - re - re me - i de - us
8 -per mi - se - re - re me - i de - us Ti -
mi - se - re - re me - i de - - us
mi - se - re - re me - i de - us
mi - se - re - re me - i de - us___

80
- bi so - li pec - ca - ui et ma - lum co - ram te fe -
Ti - - bi so - li pec - ca - ui et ma - lum co - ram te
85
- ci ut iu - sti - fi - ce - ris in ser - mo - ni - bus tu - is et uin - cas
fe - ci ut iu - sti - fi - ce - ris in ser - mo - ni - bus tu - is et uin -
90
mi - se - re -
cum iu - di - ca - ris mi -
mi - se - re - re me - i
- cas cum iu - di - ca - ris mi - se - re - re
mi - se - re - re me -

95
-re me - i de - us ec - - ce e - nim *in*
- se - re - re me - i de - us ec - ce e - nim *in*
de - us
me - i de - - us ec - ce e - nim *in*
- i de - - us ec - ce e - nim *in*
100
in - i - - qui - ta - ti - bus con - ce - ptus sum
in - i - qui - ta - - ti - bus con - ce - ptus sum *con* -
in - i - qui - ta - ti - bus con - ce - ptus sum
in - i - qui - ta - ti - bus con - ce - ptus sum con -
105
et in pec - ca - tis *con - ce - pit me* ma -
- *ce* - *ptus* *sum* con - ce - ptus sum
et in pec - ca - tis con - ce - pit me ma - ter me -
- ce - ptus sum et in pec - ca - tis con - ce - pit me

110
- ter me - - a mi - - se - re - re me -
mi - se - re - re me - i de - -
mi - se - re - re me - i de - -
- a mi - se - re - re me - i
ma - ter me - - a mi - se - re - re me - i
115
- i de - - us ec - ce e - nim ue -
- - us ec - ce e - nim ue -
- us
de - - us ec - ce e - nim
de - - us
120
- ri - ta - tem di - - le - xi - Sti in - cer - ta
- ri - ta - tem di - - le - xsi - Sti in - cer - ta
ue - ri - ta - tem di - le - Xi - sti in - cer -

125
et o - cul - ta sa - pi - en - ti - e tu - e
et o - cul - ta sa - pi - en - ti - e tu - e
- ta et o - cul - ta sa - - pi - en - ti - e tu -
130
ma - ni - - fe - sta - sti mi - - - -
ma - ni - - fe - sta - sti mi - - - chi
- e ma - ni - fe - sta - sti mi - - -
135
- chi mi - se - re - re me - i de - -
mi - - se - re - re me - i de - - -
mi - se - re - re me - i de - us
- hi mi - - se - re - re me - i de -
Mi - se - re - re me - i de - - us

140
- us a - sper - ges me do - mi -
- us
- us a - sper - ges me do - - - mi -
145
- ne y - so - po
a - sper - ges me do - - mi - ne hy - so -
- ne
a - sper - ges me do - - - mi - ne y -
150
et mun - da - - - bor la -
- po y - so - po et mun - da - - bor la -
y - so - po et mun - da - - bor
- so - po et mun - da - bor la - ua - bis me

155
-ua - bis me et su - per ni - uem de - - al -
-ua - bis me *la - va - - bis me* et su - per ni - uem
La - ua - bis me et su - per ni - uem de - al -
et su - per ni - - uem de -
160
- ba - - bor mi - se - re - re me - i de -
de - al - ba - bor mi - - se - re - re
mi - se - re - re me - i
- - - ba - - bor mi - - se - re - re
- al - ba - bor mi - se - re - re
165
- - - - - us.
me - i de - us.
de - - us.
me - i de - - us.
me - i de - - us.

[Secunda pars]
5
Au - di
au - di - tu - i me - o da - bis
Au - di
au - di - tu - i me -
10
gau - di - um et le - - ti - ci-am et ex - ul - ta - bunt os -
- o da - bis gau - di - um et le - ti - ci - am et ex - ul -
15
Mi - se - re - re me - i
Mi - se -
Mi - se - re - re
- - sa hu - - mi - li - a - - ta
- ta - bunt os - - sa hu - mi - li - a - ta

20
de - - - us a - uer - te fa - ci - em
re - re me - i de - us a - uer - te fa - ci - em tu - am
me - i de - us
a - uer - te fa - ci - em tu -
a - uer - te fa - ci - em tu - am
25
tu - am a pe - ca - tis me - is et o - mnes in -
a pec - ca - tis me - is et o - mnes in - i - qui -
am a pec - ca - tis me - is et o - mnes in - i - qui -
a pec - ca - tis me - is et o - mnes in - i - qui -
30
i - qui - ta - tes me - as de - - le
ta - tes me - as de - le
mi - se - re - re
ta - tes me - - as de - le mi - se - re - re
ta - tes me - as de - le mi - se - re - re

35
cor mun - dum cre - a in me de -
cor mun - dum cre - a in me
me - i de - us
me - i de - us
me - i de - us
40
- us et spi - ri - tum re - ctum in -
de - us et spi - ri - tum re - ctum in - no -
45
- no - ua in ui - sce - ri - bus me - is mi - se - re - re
- ua in ui - sce - ri - bus me - is mi - se - re - re
mi - se - re - re
mi - se -
mi - se - re - re

50
me - i De - - us
me - i De - - us
me - i de - us
- re - re Me - i de - us ne pro - i - ci - as me a fa - ci -
me - i De - us ne pro - i - ci - as me a
55
- e tu - a et spi - ri - tum san - ctum tu - um ne au -
fa - ci - e tu - a et spi - ri - tum san - ctum tu - um ne au - fe -
60
mi - se - re - re me - i de - us
mi - se - re - re me - i de - us
- fe - ras a me mi - se - re - re me - i de - us red -
- ras a me mi - se - re - re me - i de - us

65
red - - de mi - chi le - ti - ci - am sa - lu -
red - de mi - chi le - ti - - ci - am sa - lu - ta -
- de mi - chi le - ti - - ci - am sa - lu - ta - - ris
red - de mi - chi le - ti - - ci - am sa - lu - ta - ris tu -
70
- ta - ris tu - i et spi - ri - tu prin - ci - pa - li
- ris tu - i et spi - - ri - tu prin - ci - pa - -
tu - - - i et spi - ri - tu prin - ci -
- - - i et spi - ri - tu prin - ci -
75
con - fir - ma me con - fir - ma me
- li con - fir - - - ma me
- pa - li con - fir - - - ma
- pa - li con - fir - - ma me con - fir - - ma me

80
do - ce - bo in - i -
mi - se - re - re me - i de - us
mi - se - re - re me - i de - us
me mi - se - re - re me - i de - us do - ce - bo in - i -
mi - se - re - re me - i de - us
85
- quos ui - as tu - - as
mi - se - re - re me - i de -
mi - se - re - re me - i de -
- quos ui - as tu - - as mi - se - re - re me - i de -
mi - se - re - re me - i de -
90
et in - pi - j ad te con - uer - ten - tur
- us et im - pi - j ad te con - uer - ten - tur
- us
- us et in - pi - j
- us et im - pi -

95
mi - se - re - re me - i de - -
mi - se - re - re me - i de - us
mi - se - re - re me - i de -
ad te con - uer - ten - tur
- j ad te con - uer - ten - tur
100
- us Li - - be - ra
li - - be - ra me de san - Gui - ni - bus
- us
Li - be - ra me
li - be - ra me de san - gui - ni - Bus
105
me de san - gui - ni - bus de - us de - us
de - us de - us sa - lu - - tis_ me -
de san - gui - ni - bus de - us de - us sa - lu - - tis_ me -
de - us de - us sa - lu - - tis_ me -

110
sa - lu - tis me - e et ex - ul - ta - bit lin - gua me -
- e et ex - ul - ta - bit lin -
- e sa - lu - - tis me - e et ex - ul - ta - bit lin -
- e et ex - ul - ta - bit lin - gua me -
115
- a iu - sti - ti - am tu - - - am mi - se - re - re
- gua me - a iu - sti - ti - am tu - - - am mi - se - re - re
mi - se - re - re
- gua me - a iu - sti - ti - am tu - am mi - se - re - re
- a iu - sti - ti - am tu - am mi - se - re - re
120
me - i de - us mi - se - re - re me - i.
me - i de - us mi - se - re - re me - i.
me - i de - us.
me - i de - us mi - se - re - re me - i.
me - i de - us. i

[Tertia pars]
Do - mi - ne La - bi - a me - a a -
Do - mi - ne la - bi - a me - a a - pe - ri -
Do - mi - ne
Do - mi - ne la - bi - a me -
5
10
- pe - ri - es et os me - um a - nun - ti - a - bit
- es et os me - um a - nun - ti - a - bit
La - bi - a me - a a - pe - ri - es et os me - um a -
- a a - pe - ri - es et os me - um a - nun - ti - a -
15
Lau - dem tu - - am
Lau - dem tu - - - am mi - - se - re - re
mi - se - re - re
- nun - ti - a - bit lau - dem tu - - am mi - se -
- bit lau - dem tu - am mi -

20
quo - - ni - am si uo - lu - ys -
me - i de - - - us
me - i de - - - us
- re - re me - i de - - us quo - ni - am si uo - lu - is -
- se - re - re me - i de - - us
25
- ses sa - - cri - fi - ci - um de - dis -
quo - ni - am si uo - lu - i - ses
- ses sa - cri - fi - ci - um de - dis -
quo - ni - am si uo - lu - is - ses
30
- sem u - ti - que o - lo - cau - stis
sa - cri - fi - ci - um de - di - sem u - ti -
- sem u - ti - que o - lo - cau -
sa - cri - fi - ci - um de - dis - sem u -

35
non de - le - cta - be - ris non
-que o - lo - cau - stis non de - le - cta - be - ris
- stis non de - le - cta - be - ris non
- ti - que ho - lo - cau - stis non de - le - cta - be - ris
40
de - le - cta - be - ris mi -
non de - le - cta - be - ris non de - le - cta - be - ris
mi - se -
de - le - cta - be - ris non de - le - cta - be - ris
non de - le - cta - be - ris non de - le - cta - be - ris
45
- se - re - re me - i de - us sa - cri - fi - ci - um de -
mi - se - re - re me - i de - us sa - cri - fi - ci -
- re - re me - i de - us
mi - se - re - re me - i de - us
mi - se - re - re me - i de - us

50
- - - o
Spi - ri -
-um de - o
Spi -
Sa - cri - fi - ci - um de - - - o
Sa - cri - fi - ci - um de - o
55
60
-tus con - tri - bu - la - - - tus
cor
-ri - tus con - tri - bu - la - tus
spi - ri -tus con - tri - bu - la - tus
spi - ri - tus con - tri - bu - la - tus
65
con - tri - tum et hu - mi - li - a - tum
cor con - - tri - tum et hu - mi - li - a - tum
cor con - - tri - tum et
cor con - tri -

70
de - - us non de - - spi - ci -
hu - mi - li - a - - tum de - - us non de - spi - ti -
- tum et hu - mi - li - a - - tum de - us non de - spi - ci -
75
de - - us non de - spi - ci - es
- es de - us non de - spi - ci -
- es de - - us non de - - spi - ci - es de - us non de - - spi - ci -
- es de - us non de - spi - ci -
80
be -
- es mi - - se - re - re me - i de - - - us
mi - se - re - re me - i de - - - us
- es mi - se - re - re me - i de - - - us be - ni -
- es mi - se - re - re me - i de - us

85
- ni - gne fac do - mi - ne in bo - na uo - lun - ta - te tu -
be- - ni - gne fac do - mi - ne
- gne fac do - mi - ne in bo - na uo - lun - ta - te tu - a sy -
be - ni - gne fac do - mi - ne
90
- a sy - on ut e - di - fi - cen-
in bo - na uo - lun - ta - te tu - a sy - on
- on ut e - di - fi -
in bo - na uo - lun - ta - te tu - a sy - on
95
100
- tur mu - ri Je - ru - sa - lem mi - se - re - re
mi - se - re - re me - i
mi - se - re - re me - i
- cen - tur mu - ri ie - ru - sa - lem mi - se - re - re me - i
mi - se - re - re

105
me - i de - - - us
tunc ac - ce -
de - - us
de - - us
de - - us tunc ac - ce - - pta - bis
tunc ac - ce - pta - bis
me - i de - us
Tunc ac - ce - - pta - bis
110
- - pta - - bis sa - cri - fi - ci - um Ju -
Tunc ac - ce - - *pta* - bis sa - cri - fi - ci - um iu -
sa - cri - fi - ci - um Ju -
tunc ac - ce - pta - - bis
Sa - cri - fi - ci - um iu -
115
- Sti - ti - e ob - la - ti - o - nes et ho - lo - cau - sta tunc
- Sti - ti - e ob - la - ti - o - nes et o - lo - cau - - sta Tunc
- Sti - ti - e ob - la - ti - o - nes et ho - lo - cau - sta tunc
- Sti - *ti* - e ob - la - ti - o - nes et o - lo - cau - sta tunc

120
im - po - nent 6) su - per al - ta - re tu - um ui - tu -
im - po - nent 7) su - per al - ta - re tu - um ui -
im - po - nent 7) su - per al - ta - re tu - um ui - tu -
im - po - nent 7) su - per al - ta - re tu - um ui - tu -
125
- los mi - se - re - re me - i de - us
- tu - los mi - se - re - re 8) me - i de - us
mi - se - re - re me - i de
- los mi - se - re - re me - i de - us
- los mi - se - re - re me - i de - us
130
135
mi - se - re - re me - i de - us.
mi - se - re - re me - i de - us.
- us.
mi - se - re - re me - i de - us.
mi - se - re - re me - i de - us.

ACOB OBRECHT *Missa Fortuna desperata:* Gloria and Credo

Gloria

Jacob Obrecht, *Collected Works.* Vol. 4. Ed. Hudson (Utrecht: Vereniging voor Nederlandse Muziekgeschiedenis, 1986), pp. 55–71.

30
Be - ne - di - - - - - - ci - mus te. Ad - o - ra - mus
Be - - - - - - - ne - di - ci - mus
te. Ad - o - - ra - mus
te. Ad - - - - o - ra -
35
te. Glo - ri - fi - ca - - - mus te. Gra -
te. Glo - ri - fi - ca - mus te.
te. Glo - ri - - - - fi - ca - mus
-mus te. Glo - ri - fi - ca - mus te, glo - ri - fi - ca - mus
40
- - - - - ti - as a - - gi - mus ti - bi
Gra - - ti - as a - gi - mus...
te. Gra - ti - as a - gi - mus ti - - bi
te. Gra - - ti - as a - gi - mus ti - bi
45
pro - pter ma - - - - gnam glo - - - - -
pro - - - pter ma - - - - gnam
pro - pter ma - - - - gnam glo - - - - -

50
- ri - am tu - - am.
glo - ri - am tu - am, tu - - - - - - - - -
- ri - am tu - am, tu - - - - - - - - - - - - -
55
Do - mi - ne De - us, De - - us, Rex
- am.
- - - am. Do - - - - - mi -
- - am. Do - mi - ne De - us, De - - us, Rex
60
65
ce - le - stis, De - us Pa - - - - - - ter o - mni -
- - - ne De - -
ce - le - stis, De - us Pa - ter o - mni - po - tens, o -
70
- po - tens. Do - mi - ne Fi - - li
Do - mi - ne Fi - li
- - us... Do - mi - ne
- mni - po - tens. Do - mi - ne

75
u - ni - ge - ni - te
Ie - su Chri - ste, Chri -
Fi - li u - ni - ge -
Fi - li u - ni - ge -
80
85
Ie - su Chri - ste.
- ste, Ie - su Chri -
-ni - te Ie - su, Ie - su Chri -
-ni - te Ie - su, Ie - su Chri - ste.
90
Do - mi - ne De - us, Do - mi -
- ste. Do - mi - ne
-ste. Do - mi - ne De - us, De -
Do - mi - ne De - us, Do - mi - ne De -
95
-ne De - us, De - us, A - gnus De - i,
De - us...
- us, A - gnus De - i,
- us, De - us, A - gnus De - i,

100
A - gnus De - i, Fi - li - us Pa - - - - - -
A - gnus De - i, Fi - li - us Pa - - - - - -
A - gnus De - i, Fi - li - us Pa - - - - - -
105
- - - tris, Pa - tris, Pa - tris, Pa - - - tris.
- - - tris, Pa - tris, Pa - - - - - - - tris.
- - - tris, Pa - tris, Pa - - - - - - - - tris.
110
Qui tol - lis pec - ca - - - - - - ta mun-
Qui
Qui tol - lis pec - - - - - ca - ta
Qui tol - - - - lis pec - ca - - ta
115
120
- di,
mun - - - - - - - - - - di, mi - se - re - re no-
mun - di, pec - ca - ta mun - di, pec - ca - ta mun - di, mi - se - re - re

125
mi - se - re - re no - bis, mi - se - re - -
mi - se - re - re no - bis, mi - se - re - -
- bis, mi - - - - se - re - re no - - bis, no -
no - bis, mi - se - re - re no - bis, mi - se - re -
130
-re no - bis.
-re no - - - - - bis.
- - - bis. Qui tol - - - - - - - - - - -
- re no - bis. Qui tol - - - - - - - - - - -
135
140
Qui tol - lis pec - ca - ta
Qui tol - lis pec - ca - ta
- - lis, qui tol - lis pec - ca - ta mun -
- lis, qui tol - lis pec -
145
mun - di, su - sci - pe de - pre - ca - tio - nem no - -
mun - di, su - - sci - pe de -
-di, su - sci - pe de - pre - ca - ti - o - nem no -
-ca - ta mun - di, su - sci - pe de - pre - ca - ti - o -

150
- stram. Qui se - des ad de - xte - ram Pa - - - - - - - tris,
-pre - ca - ti - o - nem...
-stram. Qui se - des ad de - xte - ram Pa - tris,
-nem no - stram. Qui se - des ad de - xte - ram Pa - tris,
155
mi - se - re - re no - - - - - bis. Quo - ni - am
mi - se - re - re no - - - bis.
mi - se - re - re no - - - - - bis. Quo - ni - am
¢
160
165
tu so - lus, tu so - lus san - ctus. Tu so - lus Do - mi - nus,
Tu
... tu so - lus, tu so - lus san - ctus, san -
tu so - lus, tu so - lus san - ctus. Tu so - lus Do - mi - nus,
170
tu so - lus Do - mi - nus, tu so - lus Do - mi - nus, tu so - lus Do - mi - nus,
- ctus. Tu so - lus Do - - - mi - nus, tu so - lus Do - mi - nus,
tu so - lus Do - mi - nus, tu so - lus Do - mi - nus, tu so - lus Do - mi - nus,

175
tu so - lus Do - mi - nus, tu so - lus Do - mi - nus. Tu so - lus
Tu so - lus Al -
tu so - lus Do - mi - nus, tu so - lus Do - mi - nus.
tu so - lus Do - mi - nus, tu so - lus Do - mi - nus.
180
Al - tis - si - mus, Ie -
- tis - si - mus, Ie -
Tu so - lus Al - tis - si - mus, Ie -
Tu so - lus Al - tis - si - mus,
185
190
- su Chri - ste, Chri - ste.
- su Chri - ste, Ie - su Chri - ste. Cum San - -
-su Chri - ste, Chri - ste. Cum San - -
Ie - su Chri - ste. Cum San - -
195
200
Spi - ri - tu, . in
- - cto Spi - - - - - - - ri - tu, in
- - cto Spi - ri - tu, in
- - cto Spi - ri - tu, in

205
210
215
glo - ri - a De - i Pa - tris, cum San - cto Spi -
glo - ri - a De - i...
glo - ri - a De - i, cum San -
glo - ri - a De - i, cum San - - cto Spi -
-ri - - - - - - tu in glo - ri - a De - i Pa - - - - -
- cto Spi - ri - tu in glo - ri - a De - i Pa - - - - -
-ri - - - - - - tu in glo - ri - a De - i Pa - - - - -
- - - tris. A - - - - - - - - - - - men.
- - - tris. A - - - - - - - - - - - men.
- - - tris. A - - - - - - - - - - - men.

Credo

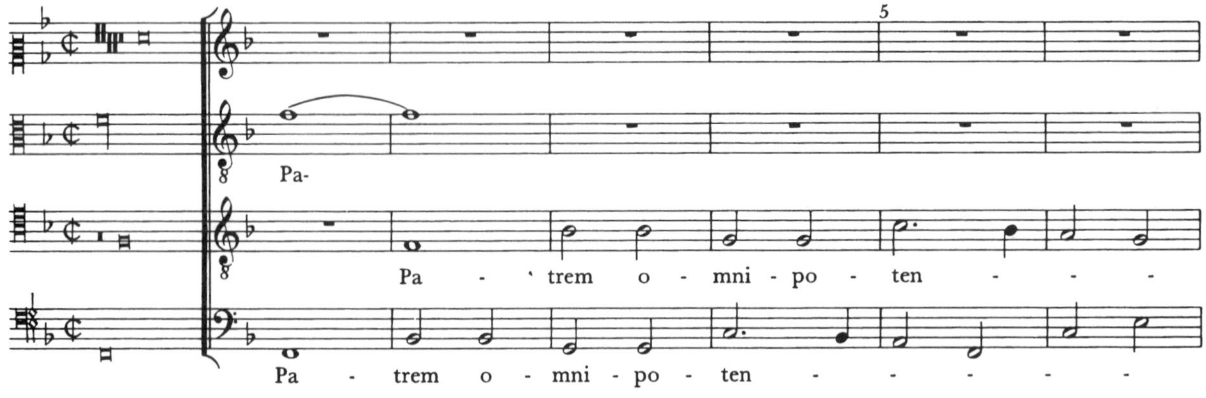
5
Pa-
Pa - trem o - mni - po - ten - - - -
Pa - trem o - mni - po - ten - - - - - - -

fa - cto - rem ce - li et
- - - - - - - - tem, fa - cto - rem
- - - - - tem, fa - cto - rem ce -
ter - - - - - re, vi - si - bi -
fa - - - - cto - rem ce - li et
ce - li et ter - re, vi - si - bi - - li -
- li et ter - re, vi - si - bi - - li -
- li - um o - mni - um, et in - vi - si -
ter - re, vi - si - bi - li - um o -
- um o - - mni - um, et in - vi - si - bi - -
- um... et in - vi - si - bi - li - um,
-bi - - - li - um. Et in u -
-mni - um, et in - vi - si - bi - li - um. Et
-li - um, o - mni - um, et in - vi - si - bi - li - um.
in - vi - si - bi - li - um. Et

35
40
- num Do - - mi-num Ie - sum Chri - - - - - - stum,
in u - num Fi -
Ie - sum Chri - - - - - - stum,
in u - num Do - mi-num Ie - sum Chri - - - - - - stum,
45
Fi - li - um De - i u - - - - ni - ge - - - - ni-
-li - um De - i
Fi - li - um De - i u - - ni - ge - ni -
Fi - li - um De - i u - - - - ni - ge - - - - ni-
50
-tum. Et ex Pa - tre na - tum an - te o -
-tum. Et ex Pa - tre na - tum an - te o - - -
-tum. Et ex Pa - tre na - tum an - te o - mni-
55
- mni - a se - cu - la.
-la...
- mni - a se - cu - la. De - - um de De -
- a se - cu - la. De - um de De -

60
65
lu - men de lu - mi - ne, De - um ve -
- - - o, lu - men de lu - mi - ne, De - um ve -
- - - o, lu - men de lu - - - - - - - mi -
70
- rum de De - o ve - ro. Ge - ni - tum, non fa -
Ge - ni - tum, non
- - - rum de De - o ve - ro. Ge - - - ni - tum, non
- ne... Ge - ni - tum, non
75
- ctum, con - sub - stan - ti - a - lem Pa - - - tri, con -
fa - ctum, con - sub - stan - ti - a - - -
fa - ctum, con - sub - stan - ti - a - lem, con - sub - stan - ti - a - lem Pa -
fa - ctum, ge - ni - tum, non fa - ctum,
80
3
- - - sub - stan - ti - a - lem Pa - - - - - - tri: per
- - - lem Pa - - - - - - - tri:
- - - tri, con - sub - stan - ti - a - lem Pa - - - - tri: per
con - sub - stan - ti - a - lem Pa - tri: per

85
quem o - mni - a fa - cta sunt.
Qui
quem o - mni - a fa - - - - cta sunt.
quem o - mni - a fa - - - - cta sunt.
90
95
Qui pro - pter nos ho - mi - nes, et pro -
pro - pter nos ho - mi - nes, et pro - pter
Qui pro - - pter nos ho - - - - mi -
Qui pro - pter nos ho - mi - nes, et pro -
100
- pter no - stram sa - lu - - - - - tem de - scen - -
no - stram
- nes... de - scen - -
- pter no - stram sa - lu - - - - - tem de - -
105
- - - dit, de - scen - - dit de ce - lis.
- dit, de - scen - dit, de - scen - dit de ce - lis.
- - - scen - dit, de - scen - dit de ce - lis.

110
115
Et in - car -
Et
Et in - car - na - tus est de
Et in - car - na - tus est de Spi - ri -
120
-na - tus est de Spi - ri - - - - tu San - - -
Spi - ri - tu San - cto ex Ma - - ri -
- tu San - cto ex Ma - ri - a, ex Ma - - ri -
125
-cto ex Ma - ri - a Vir - gi - ne: Et ho - mo
Et ho - - - - - - - mo
- a Vir - gi - ne: Et ho - - - - - -
- a Vir - gi - ne: Et ho - - - - - - mo
130
135
fa - ctus est.
fa - ctus est. Cru - ci - fi - xus e -
-mo fa - - ctus est. Cru - ci - fi - xus e -
fa - ctus est. Cru - ci - fi - xus e -

140
et se - pul - tus
-ti - am pro no - bis: sub Pon - ti - o Pi - la -
-ti - am pro no - bis: sub Pon - ti - o Pi - la - to pas - sus, et se -
-ti - am pro no - bis: sub Pon - ti - o Pi - la - to pas - sus, et se - pul -
145
150
est. Et re - sur - re - xit ter - ti - a di - e, se - - -
- - - to... Et a -
-pul - tus est. Et re - sur - re - xit ter - ti - a di - e... Et a - scen -
-tus est. Et re - sur - re - xit ter - ti - a di - e.
155
-cun - dum Scri - ptu - ras. Et i - te - rum ven-
-scen - - - dit
- dit in ce - lum: se - det ad de - xte-ram Pa - - tris. Et
Et a - scen - dit in ce - lum: se - det ad de - xte-ram Pa - tris. Et
160
- tu - - rus est cum glo - ri - a, iu - di - ca - - re
i - te - rum... cum glo - ri - a, iu - di - ca - re vi -
i - te - rum... cum glo - ri - a, iu - di - ca - -

165
vi - vos et mor - tu - os: cu - ius re - gni non e - rit fi -
vi...
-vos et mor - tu - os:
-re... cu - ius re - gni non e - rit fi -
170
175
- nis. Et in Spi - ri - tum San - ctum, Do - mi - num,
Et in Spi - - - - ri - tum San - ctum, Do - mi - num, et
-nis. Et in Spi - ri - tum San - ctum, Do - mi - num, et
180
et vi - vi - fi - can - tem... Con - fi - te - or u - - -
Con - fi - - - - - te - -
vi - vi - fi - can - tem... Con - fi - te -
vi - vi - fi - can - tem... Con - fi - - - - te - or u -
185
- num ba - ptis - ma in re - mis - si - o - nem pec -
- or u - num ba - ptis - - - ma in re -
- or u - num ba - ptis - ma in re - mis - si - o - nem pec-
- num ba - ptis-ma in re - - - mis - si - o - nem pec -

190
195
-ca - to - rum.
-mis - si - o - nem...
- ca - to - rum. Et ex - spe - cto re - sur - re - cti - o - -
-ca - to - rum. Et ex - spe - cto re - sur - re - cti - o - -
200
Et vi - - tam ven - tu - - - - - -
Et vi - tam ven - tu - - -
- - - nem mor - tu - o - rum. Et vi - tam
- - - nem mor - tu - o - - - - rum. Et
205
210
-ri se - - cu - li, se - - - - - - - - cu -
-ri se - cu - li.
ven - tu - - - - ri se - - - - - - - - -
vi - tam ven - tu - ri se - - - - - - - - -
3
215
-li. A - - - - - - - - - - - - - men.
- - - - - cu - li. A - men, a - - - - - - men.
- - - - cu - li. A - - - - - - - - - - - - men.

42 JOSQUIN DESPREZ *Missa Pange lingua:* Kyrie*

Josquin Desprez, *Werken.* Missen 4. Ed. Smijers (Amsterdam: Vereniging voor Nederlandse Muziekgeschiedenis, 1952), pp. 1–3. 219

20
Chri - ste, Chri - ste
Chri - ste, Chri - ste
25
30
Chri - ste, Chri -
Chri - ste, Chri - ste
35
ste
e - lei -
Chri - ste
e - lei -
40
e - lei -
son, e - lei -
e -
son, e - lei -

son
son, e - lei - son
lei - son, e - lei - son.
son, e - lei - son
Ky-ri-e e - lei - son,
Ky - ri-e e - lei - son,
Ky - ri-e e - lei
Ky - ri-e
Ky - ri - e, Ky - ri - e, Ky - ri - e
Ky - ri - e, Ky - ri - e, Ky - ri - e
son, Ky - ri - e e - lei
e - lei - son, Ky - ri - e
e - lei - son
e - lei - son, e - leí - son.
son
e - lei - son, Ky - ri - e e - le - i - son.

43 PIERRE DE LA RUE *Missa pro defunctis:* Introitus

Te de-cet hy-mnus, De-us in Si-on,
20
Et ti-bi red-de-tur vo-tum in Je-
Et ti-bi red-de-tur vo-tum in Je-
Et ti-bi red-de-tur vo-tum in
Et ti-bi red-de-tur vo-tum in Je-
25
-ru-sa-lem: Ex-au-di o-ra-ti-o-nem me-
-ru-sa-lem: Ex-au-di, De-us, o-ra-ti-
Je-ru-sa-lem: Ex-au-di o-ra-ti-o-nem
-ru-sa-lem: Ex-au-di o-ra-ti-o-nem me-
30
-am, ad te o-mnis ca-ro ve-ni-et.
-o-nem me-am, ad te o-mnis ca-ro ve-ni-et.
me-am, ad te o-mnis ca-ro ve-ni-et.
-am, ad te o-mnis ca-ro ve-ni-et.

44 HEINRICH ISAAC *Missa de apostolis:* Kyrie

14
ri - e e
ri - e e
Ky - ri - e e - lei - son, e
ri - e e - lei - son, e
e - lei - son,
e - lei - son,
20
lei - son, e - lei - son.
lei - son, e - lei - son.
lei - son.
lei - son, e - lei - son.
e - lei - son, e - lei - son.
e - lei - son, e - lei - son.
Ky - ri - e lei - son.
26
Chri - ste, Chri - ste e
Chri - ste
Chri - ste, Chri - ste
Chri - ste, Chri
Chri - ste, Chri
Chri

35
lei - - - - son, Chri -
e - - - - lei - - - - son, Chri -
e - - - - - lei - - - - - - - son,
ste e - - - lei - - - - son,
ste e - lei - - - - - son, e - lei - - - son,
ste e - lei - son, e - lei - son,
44
ste e - - - lei - - - son.
ste e - - - - lei - - - son.
e - lei - - son, e - - - - - - lei - son.
Chri - - - - ste e - - - lei - son.
Chri - - - - ste e - - - - - lei - son.
e - lei - son, e - - - lei - son.
Chri - ste lei - son.
53
Chri - - - - - - - ste, Chri - - ste e - lei -
Chri - - - - - - - - ste
Chri - - - - - ste e - lei - son, Chri - - ste e - lei -
Chri - - - - - - - ste e - lei - - - - - son, Chri - - - ste
Chri - ste e - lei - - - - - son, Chri - ste e -
Chri - - - - - - ste,

62
son, Chri - - - - - - - - - - - - ste
e -
son, Chri - - - - - ste e - lei - -
e - lei - son, Chri - - - - - - - - - - ste
lei - - - - - son, Chri - - - - - - - - - ste e - lei - -
Chri - - - - - - - - - ste e - lei - -
71
e - lei - - - - - - son, son.
lei - - - - - - son, e - - - - - - lei - son.
son, e - lei - son, e - - - - - - lei - son.
e - - - lei - - son, e - - - - - - lei - - - - son.
son, e - lei - - - - son, e - - - - lei - - - - son.
son, e - - - - - - - lei - son.
Ky - - - - - - - - - ri - e lei - son.
80
Ky - - - - - - - - - - - - - - -
Ky - - - - - - - - - - - ri - e e - lei - - -
Ky - - - - - - - - - - - - ri - e e - - - -
Ky - - - - - - - - - - - -
Ky - - - - - - - - - - - - - -
Ky - - - - - - - - - - - - - -

86
ri - e e - lei -
son, Ky - ri - e e - lei - son,
lei - son, Ky - ri - e e -
ri - e, Ky - ri - e e - lei -
ri - e, Ky - ri - e
92
son, Ky - ri - e e -
e - lei - son, Ky-ri - e e - lei - son,
lei - son, Ky - ri - e e - lei -
ri - e e - lei - son, e - lei -
son, Ky - ri - e e -
e - lei - son, Ky - ri - e e - lei - son,
98
lei - son, Ky - ri -
e - lei - son, Ky - ri - e e -
son, Ky - ri - e
son, e - lei - son, Ky - ri -
lei - son, e - lei - son, Ky -
e - lei - son,

103
e e - lei - - - - - - - - - - - - - - - son.
lei - - - - - - - - son, e - lei - - - - - - son.
e - lei - - - - - - - - son.
e - e - lei - - - - - - - - - - - - son.
ri - - - - e e - lei - - - - - son.
e - lei - - - - - - - - - - - - - son.

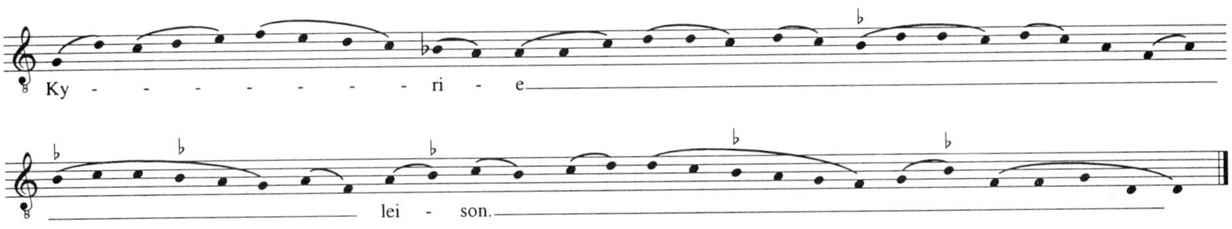
Ky - - - - - - - - ri - e
lei - son.

45 LOYSET COMPÈRE *Venes, regretz*

A celle fin que mon cueur sente et pleure
Le mal qu'il a et en quoy il labeure
Je suis contraint vous ouvrir la grant porte.
Venes, regretz . . .

Mais gardez bien qu'après vous ne demeure
L'abit de dueil plus noir que belle meure
Plain de larmes affin que je la porte
Ne tardez plus car mon sens se transporte
Si vous voulez me voyr ains que je meure.
Venes, regretz . . .

46 JOSQUIN DESPREZ *Plus nulz regretz*

20
criptz. O - res re -
O - res re - vient
criptz. O - res re - vient le bon temps Sa - tur -
O - res re - vient le bon temps Sa - tur - - -
25
vient le bon temps Sa - tur - - nus Ou
le bon temps Sa - tur - nus Ou peu con -
- - - nus Ou peu con - gnuz
nus Ou peu con - gnuz
30
peu con - gnuz fu - rent plain-tifs
gnuz fu - rent plain - tifs et cris, fu - rent plain-tifs et
fu - rent plain-tifs et cris, (fu - rent plain-
fu - rent plain-tifs et cris, (fu - rent plain-tifs et

35
— et — cris. Long temps nous ont
cris. Long temps nous ont tous
tifs et cris.) Long temps nous ont —
cris.) Long temps nous ont tous mal-heurs
40
tous mal - heurs in - fi - niz
mal-heurs in - fi - niz — Ba- tuz,
— tous mal-heurs in - fi - niz
in - fi - niz Ba - tuz pu -
45
Ba - tuz, pu - gniz et fais po - vres mai -
pu - gniz — et fais po - vres mai - gretz, —
Ba - tuz, pu - gniz — et
gniz et fais po - vres mai -

50
gretz, (et fais po - vres mai -
(et fais po - vres mai - - -
fais po - vres mai - gretz, (et
gretz, (et fais po - vres mai -
55
gretz;) Mais main - te - nant d'es -
- gretz;) Mais main - te - nant d'es - poir som -
fais po - vres mai - gretz;) Mais main - te -
gretz;) Mais main - te - nant d'es -
60
poir som - mes gar - - - niz; Joinctz
mes gar - - - niz; Joinctz et u -
nant d'es - poir som - mes gar - niz; Joinctz
poir som - mes gar - niz; Joinctz et u -

Sur noz preaux et jardinetz herbus
Luyra Phebus de ses rais ennobliz;
Ainsy croistront noz boutoneaux barbus,
Sans nulz abus et dangereux troubliz.

Regretz plus nulz ne nous viennent apres:
Nostre eure est pres, venant des cieulx beniz.
Voisent ailleurs regretz plus durs que gretz,
Fiers et aigretz, et charchent autres nidz!

Se Mars nous tolt la blanche fleur de lis
Sans nulz delictz, sy nous donne Venus
Rose vermeille, amoureuse, de pris,
Dont noz espritz n'auront regretz plus nulz.

47 PIERRE DE LA RUE *Pourquoy non*

20
quoy non
(pour – quoy non)
Pour – quoy non
Pour – quoy non
25
30
ne doy je que – – rir, (que-rir, que –
ne doy je que - rir ne doy je que –
ne doy je que – rir, (que - rir, que – –
ne doy je que – rir, ne doy je que –
35
– – – – rir) La fin de ma dou –
rir, La fin
– – – – rir) La fin de
– – – – rir La fin de

40
len - te vi - - - -
de ma dou - len - te vi - e,
ma dou - len - te vi -
ma dou - len - - te vi - e
45
- e, Quant j'ai-me qui
Quant j'ai - - me
- e, Quant
Quant j'ai-me qui ne m'ai - me my - e,
50
ne m'ai - me my - e, (Quant j'ai - me
(j'ai - me qui ne
j'ai - me,
(Quant j'ai - me qui ne m'ai - me

55
qui ne m'ai - me mye) Et sers sans guer - -
m'ai - me my - e Et sers
Quant j'ai - me qui ne m'ai - me my - e
mye) Et sers sans guer - don ac - que - -
60
- - don ac - que - rir, sans
sans guer - don ac - que - rir, (ac -
Et sers sans guer - don ac - que -
rir, guer - don, Et sers sans guer -
65
guer - don ac - - que - - rir?
que - rir,) sans guer - don ac-que - rir?
rir, sans guer - don ac - - que - - rir?
don ac - que - rir, (guer - don ac - que - rir?)

48 NINOT LE PETIT *Et la la la*

20
la la la Faic - tez luy bon - ne chie - re A la bel - le ber - gè - re.
la la Faic - tez luy bon - ne chie - re A la bel - le ber - gè - re.
la la la Faic - tez luy bon - ne chie - re A la bel - le ber - gè - re.
la la la Faic - tez luy bon - ne chie - re A la bel - le ber - gère.
25
M'en en - tray en no jar - din Pour
M'en en - tray en no jar - din Pour cœul - lier, pour
M'en en - tray en no jar -
M'en en - tray en no jar - din Pour cœul - lier gi - rouf - flé - e.
30
cœul - lier gi - rouf - flé - e.
cœul - lier gi - rouf - flé - e, gi - rouf - flé -
din Pour cœuil - lier gi - rouf - flé - e. La trou-vay ly
35
La trou-vay ly mien a - my Qui
e. La trou - vay ly mien a - my Qui l'a - voit
mien a - my Qui l'a - voit a - mas - sé - e, a - mas -
La trou - vay ly mien a - my Qui l'a - voit a - mas - sé -

40
l'a - voit a - mas - sé - e. Et la la la la la la la Faic -
a - mas - sé - e. La la la la la la Faic -
sé - - e. La la la la la Faic -
- - e. La la la la la la la Faic -
45
tez luy bon - ne chie - re A la bel - le ber - gè - re.
tez luy bon - ne chie - re A la bel - le ber - gè - re.
tez luy bon - ne chie - re A la bel - le ber - gè - re.
tez luy bon - ne chie - re A la bel - le ber - gè - re.

49 JOSQUIN DESPREZ *Baisés moy*

 Helen Hewitt, ed., *Canti B.* In Monuments of Renaissance Music 2 (Chicago: University of Chicago Press, 1967), pp. 186–87.

20
- e." "Non fe - ray.
fe - ray.
"Et pour - quoy?" "Se je fai - sois
pour - quoy?" "Se je fai - sois la fol -
25
Ma mè - re se - roit mar -
Ma mè - re se - roit mar - ri - -
la fol - li - - e, Ma mè - re se -
- li - - - e, Ma mè - re se - roit mar -
30
- ri - - e." "Ve - - la de
3)
- e." "Ve - la de quoy!
- roit mar - ri - - e." "Ve - la de
- ri - - e." "Ve - la de quoy!
35
quoy! ve - la de quoy!"
4)
ve - la de quoy!"
quoy! ve - la de quoy!"
ve - la de quoy!"

50 JOSQUIN DESPREZ *Faulte d'argent*

 Josquin Desprez, *Werken.* Wereldlijke Werken I. Ed. Smijers (Amsterdam: G. Alsbach, 1925), pp. 38–40.

19
c'est dou - leur non pa-reil - le. Se je le dis,
dou-leur non pa - reil - le. Se
-reil - le, c'est dou - leur non pa-reil - - - - - - le. Se
- - - - le, c'est dou-leur non pa - reil - le.
-le, c'est dou - leur non pa-reil - le.
25
se je le dis, se je le dis, las,
je le dis, se je le dis, las,
je le dis, se je le dis, se je le dis, se je le dis,
Se je le dis, se je le dis,
Se je le dis, se je le dis, se je le dis, se je le dis,
31
je scay bien pour-quoy. Sans de qui -
je scay bien pour - quoy. Sans de qui - bus il
las, je scay bien pour - quoy, pour - - - quoy. Sans
las, je scay bien pour - quoy.
las, je scay bien pour - quoy, bien

37
- - - bus, sans de qui - bus, sans de qui - bus il se fault te - nir
se fault te - nir quoy, il se fault te - nir quoy.
de qui - bus il se fault te - nir quoy, il se fault te - nir
Sans de qui - bus il se fault te - nir quoy, il se fault te - nir
pour - - - quoy. Sans de qui - - - - bus il se fault te - nir
43
-quoy. Fem -
-quoy. Fem - me qui dort pour ar - gent se res - veil - - - le,
-quoy.
-quoy. Fem - me qui dort pour ar - - gent se res - veil - le, Fem -
49
-me qui dort pour ar - gent se res - veil - - - le, se
Fem - me qui dort pour ar - gent se res - veil -
pour ar - gent se res - veil - - - - - - -
Fem - me qui dort
- me qui dort pour ar - gent se res - veil - le, res - veil - le,

55
res- veil - le, pour ar - gent se res - veil - le,
-le, pour ar - gent se res - veil - le,
-le, pour ar - gent se res- veil - le, se res - veil - le, pour
pour ar - gent se res - veil - - - le, pour ar - gent
pour ar - gent se res - veil - le, pour ar - gent
61
pour ar - gent se res- veil - le, pour
pour ar - gent se res - veil - le, pour ar - gent se res -
ar - gent se res - veil - le, pour ar - gent se res- veil - - - le,
se res - veil - - - le, pour ar - gent se res - veil -
se res - veil - le, pour ar - gent se res- veil -
67
ar - gent se res - - - - veil - - - - - le.
-veil - - - - le.
pour ar - gent se res - - - - - veil - le.
-le, pour ar - gent se res - veil - - - - - le.
- - - le, se res - - - - - - - - - veil - le.

51 MARCHETTO CARA *Ala absentia*

 William Prizer, *Courtly pastimes* (Ann Arbor, MI: UMI Research Press, 1980), pp. 363–67.

20
Lei pro - - mis - se et io iu - ra - i Al - tri
Lei promisse
Lei promisse
Lei promisse
25
più mai non a - ma - re si che don - na al
30
mon - - do ma - - i Po - trà lei far - me la - scia - re
35
Che fa el spir - to vi - - vo ogn'ho - - ra Hor cus - si

40
lon-tan a tor-to. Sol la fe che
Sol la fe che
Sol la fe
Sol la fe che mia
45
mia si gno ra M'ha pro-mes so o vi vo
mia si gno ra M'ha pro-mes
che mia si gno ra M'ha pro-mes so o
si gno ra M'ha pro mes so
50
o vi vo o mor to.
so o vi vo o mor to.
vi vo o mor to.
o vi vo o mor to.

52 ALESSANDRO COPPINI *Canto di zingane*

Joseph J. Gallucci, Jr., ed., *Florentine Festival Music 1480–1520*, Recent Researches in the Music of the Renaissance, vol. 40 (Madison, WI: A-R Editions, Inc., 1981), pp. 94–95.

Di paesi lontani et di stran locho,
lasse, venute siàno appocho appocho,
sol per darvi diletto, festa et giocho,
se carità darete a noi meschine.

Ècci fra noi chi ha buon naturale
in lavorar di mano e 'ngegnio tale
che nessun'altra a noi saria equale;
dunque pietà prendete i' noi meschine.

Buona ventura udir da noi potrete,
se 'l vostro sopra 'l nostro metterete,
la man, dico, leggiadra: intenderete
di vostro corso dal principio al fine.

Di sonar, di danzar usiàno ognora
con chi vorrà di voi; farènvi ancora
un guocho: "che l'è drento et che l'è fora,"
che suave piacer porge nel fine.

Però, care madonne, aprite porte,
le qual chiuse tenete, strette et forte,
prima che sopravengha in voi la morte,
prender piacer di noi pover' tapine.

53 JOSQUIN DESPREZ *El grillo*

Josquin Desprez, *Werken*. Wereldlijke Werken II/5. Ed. Smijers et al. (Amsterdam: Vereniging voor Nederlandse Muziekgeschiedenis, 1968), pp. 14–15.

25
to - re. Ma non fa co - me gli al - tri uc - cel - li, Co - me li han can -
Van' de fat - to in al - tro lo - co, Sem - pre el gril - lo
ta - to un po - co,
sta pur sal - do.
30
Quan - do la mag - gior el cal - do Al -
35
a capite
hor can - ta sol per a - mo - re.
re, a - mo - re, a - mo - re.
mo - re, per a - mo - re.

54 PEDRO ESCOBAR *Passame por Dios barquero*

(2)
(3)
1. Pas - sa - me por Dios bar - que - ro, da - quel - la par - te del ri - o,
4. No quie - ras mi per - di - cion pues en tu bon - dad con - fi - o
(4)
(5)
(6)
Fine
due - le - te del a - mor mi - o.
(7)
(8)
(10)
2. Que si po - nes di - la - cion en ve - nir a so - cor - rer - me
3. No po - drás des - pues va - ler - me se - gun cre - ce mi pas - sion.
D.C.

© 1987 American Institute of Musicology / Hänssler-Verlag, Neuhausen Stuttgart: Escobar, *Pasame por Dios barquero*. In *The Elvas Songbook*. Ed. Gil Miranda. In Corpus Mensurabilis Musicae 98, p. 59.

55 JUAN DEL ENCINA *Una sañosa porfia*

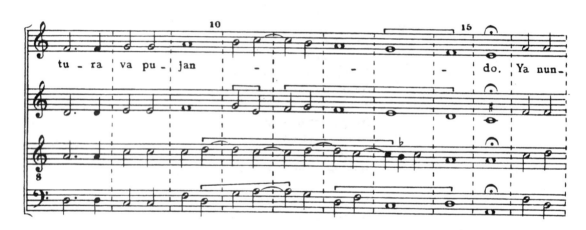

 Higinio Angles, ed., *La Música en la Corte de las Reyes Catolicos: Politonia profana—Canciones musical de Palacio.* Vol. 1, part 2. In *Monumentos de la Musica Española* 5 (Barcelona: Consejo Superior de Investigaciones Científicas, 1947), pp. 151–52.

Ya fortuna disponía
Quitar mi próspero mando,
Qu'el bravo león d'España
Mal me viene amenasando.

Córreme la morería,
Los campos viene talando,
Mis compañas i caudillos
Viene vençiendo i matando.

Una generosa Virgen
Esfuerço les viene dando;
Un famoso caballero
Delante viene volando,

Con una crus colorada
Yun espada rrelumbrando,
D'un rrico manto vestido,
Toda la gente guiando.

56 HEINRICH FINCK *Ich stund an einem morgen*

Heinrich Finck, *Ausgewahlte Werke.* Vol. 2. Eds. Hoffman Erbrecht and Lomnitzer. In *Das Erbe Deutscher Musik* 70 (Frankfürt: C. F. Peters, 1981). By permission of C. F. Peters Corporation.

- - - - gen, ver - - - - por - - - - - gen. Ich hort viel
- - gen, ver - por - - - - gen. Ich hort viel kläg - li - - -
ver - por - - - gen. Ich hort viel kläg -
- - - - gen. Ich hort viel kläg - - - li - cher Wort
kläg - li - - cher Wort von ei - - - - - nem Fräu -
- - - - cher Wort von
li - - cher Wort von ei - - nem Fräu - - lein,
von ei - - - - - - - nem Fräu - - - -
- - - - lein, was hübsch und fein, sie sprach zu ih - - rem
ei - nem Fräu - lein, was hübsch und fein, sie sprach zu ih - rem Bůh - - -
was hübsch und fein, sie sprach zu ih - - rem
- - lein, was hübsch und fein, sie sprach zu ih - - -

II ,Herzlieb, ich hab vernummen,
du wollst von hinnen schier.

Wenn wiltu wieder kummen?
Das soltu sagen mir.'

„Merk, feines Lieb, was ich dir sag:
mein Zůkunft *tůst* mich *fragen*,
weiß weder Stund noch Tag."

III Das Maidlein weinet sehre,
ihr Herz was Unmuts voll:

,So gib mir Weis und Lehre,
wie ich mich halten soll!

Für dich setz ich mein Gůt und Hab,
und wiltu hie beleiben,
ich verzehr dich Jahr und Tag.'

IV Der Knab der sprach aus Můte:
„Dein Willen ich wohl spür.

So ich verzehr dein Gůte,
ein Jahr wär bald hinfür,

dennocht müßt es geschieden sein.
Ich will dich freundlich bitten,
setz deinen Willen drein!"

V Das Freilein das schrei: ,Morte!
Mord über alles Leid!

Mich kränken deine Worte,
Herzlieb, von mir nit scheid!

57 HEINRICH ISAAC *Innsbruck, ich muss dich lassen*

Gross Leid muss ich jetzt tragen,
das ich allein tu klagen
dem liebsten Buhlen mein.
Ach Lieb, nun lass mich Armen
im Herzen dein erbarmen,
dass ich muss dannen sein.

Mein Trost ob allen Weiben,
dein tu ich ewig bleiben,
stet treu, der Ehren fromm.
Nun muss dich Gott bewahren,
in aller Tugend sparen,
bis dass ich wiederkomm.

58 JOHANNES GHISELIN *La Alfonsina*

35
40
45
50
55
60

59 ARNOLT SCHLICK *Maria zart von edler art*

24
29
34
39
43

48

52

60 ANONYMOUS Ricercar No. 2 from *Capirola Lute Book*

 Otto Gombosi, ed., *Capirola Lute Book: Compositions di Meser Vincenzo Capirola* (Neuilly-sur-Seine: Societé de Musique d'Autrefois, 1955), pp. 7–9.

6
4
7
4
tr
tr
5
4
4
4
tr
1
4

60 ANONYMOUS Ricercar No. 2 from *Capirola Lute Book*

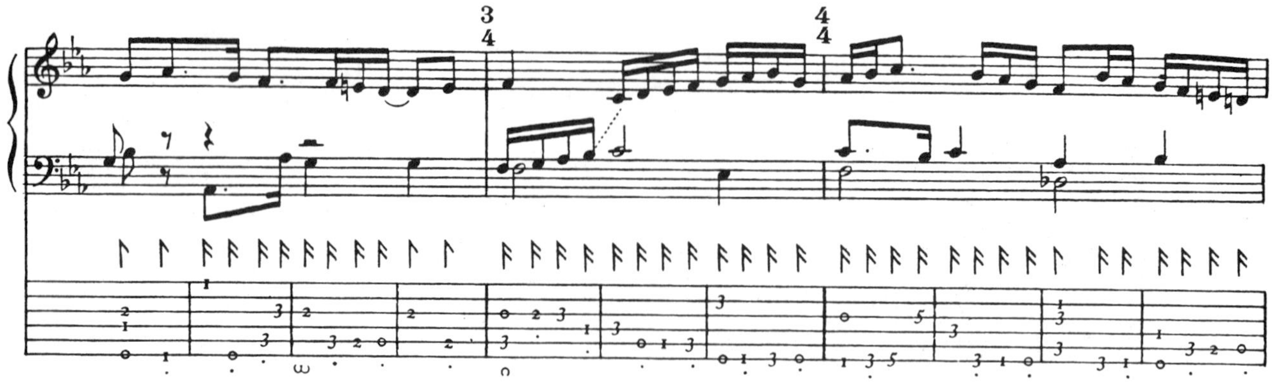

61 NICOLAS GOMBERT *Quem dicunt homines*

20
Re-spon-dens Pe - trus di - xit e - - i: Tu es Chri-
Re - spon-dens Pe - trus, re-spon-dens Pe - trus di - xit: Tu es Chri-stus fi - li-
- trus di - - xit e - i:
i, di - xit e - i, di- xit e - i: Tu es Chri - stus fi -
xit, di - xit, re - spon-dens Pe - trus di - xit e - i:
di - xit, re - spon-dens Pe-trus di - xit:
25
stus fi - li - us De - i, tu es Chri-stus fi - li - us De-i vi - vi.
us De - i vi - vi, fi - li - us De-i vi - vi.
Tu es Chri-stus fi - li - us, tu es Chri-stus fi - li-us De - i vi - vi, De-
- li - us De - i, tu es Chri-stus fi - li - us De - i vi-
Tu es Chri-stus fi - li - us De - i vi - vi. Et
Tu es Chri-stus fi - li - us De - i, fi - li - us De-
30
Et a - it Ie - sus, et a - it Ie - sus, et a - it
Et a - it Ie - sus, et a - it Ie - sus,
i vi - vi. Et a - it Ie - sus, et a - it Ie - sus, et
vi Et a - it il - li Ie - sus, et a - it il-
a - it il - li Ie - sus, et a - it Ie -
i vi - vi. Et a - it Ie - sus,

35
40
Ie - - - sus: Be-a-tus es Si-mon Ba-
et a-it Ie - sus: Be-a-tus es Si-mon Ba-rio - na,
a - it Ie - - sus: Be- a-tus es Si-
li Ie - - sus: Be- a-tus es Si - mon Ba-rio - na,
sus: Be - a-tus es Si - - mon Ba-rio -
et a-it Ie - sus: Be - a-tus es Si-mon Ba - rio-
45
rio - na qui - a ca-ro et san - guis,
be - a - tus es Si - mon Ba - rio-na qui-a ca-
mon Ba-rio - na, be - a-tus es Si - mon Ba-rio - - na qui-
be - a-tus es Si - mon Ba - rio - na, Si -
- na, be-a-tus es Si - mon Ba - rio - na qui-a ca-
- - na, be - a-tus es Si - mon Ba-rio - na
50
qui - a ca-ro et san - - guis
ro et san - guis, qui - a ca - ro et san - guis
a ca-ro et san-guis,qui- a ca-ro, qui- a ca-ro et san - -
mon Ba - rio - na qui- a ca-ro et san -
ro, qui - a ca-ro et san- guis, qui - a ca - ro et san -
qui- a ca - ro et san-guis, et san - -

55
non re- ve- la - vit ti - bi sed pa- ter
non re- ve- la - vit, non re - ve- la- vit, non re - ve- la- vit ti - bi sed
guis non re - ve- la - vit ti - - bi sed pa- ter me -
guis non re - ve - la - vit, non re - ve - la - vit ti - -
guis non re - ve- la - vit, non re - ve - la - vit ti-
guis non re - ve- la - vit ti - -
60
me - us, sed pa- ter me - us qui est in coe -
pa - ter me - us, sed pa- ter me - - us, sed pa- ter
- us, sed pa - ter me - - us qui est in coe - lis, qui
- bi sed pa - ter me - us qui est in coe - lis
bi sed pa- ter me - us qui est in coe - lis, qui
bi sed pa - ter me - us qui est in coe - lis, qui est in coe - lis,
65
70
lis Et e - go di- co ti-
me - us qui est in coe - lis. Et e - go di- co ti-
est in coe - lis, qui - est in coe - lis. Et e-
qui est in coe - lis. Et e - go di - co ti - bi, di - co
est in coe - lis, qui est in coe - lis. Et e - go di - co ti - bi,
qui est in coe - lis, qui est in coe - - lis.

bi qui - a tu es Pe - trus, qui - a tu es Pe-
bi qui- a tu es Pe-trus, es Pe - trus, qui -
go di - co ti - bi, ti - bi qui- a tu es Pe - trus,
ti - bi, di - co ti - bi qui- a tu es Pe-trus, qui- a tu es Pe-
et e - go di - co ti - bi qui- a tu es Pe-trus, qui-
Et e - go di - co ti - bi qui- a tu es
trus et su- per hanc pe - tram, et su-per hanc pe -
a tu es Pe - trus, Pe - trus et su - per hanc pe-tram,
qui - a tu es Pe-trus et su-per hanc pe - tram,
trus, es Pe-trus, qui - a tu es Pe - trus et su- per hanc pe -
a tu es Pe - trus, qui- a tu es Pe - trus et su - per hanc pe-
Pe - - trus et su-per hanc pe - - -
- - - tram ae- di- fi - ca - -
et su - per hanc pe-tram ae - di - fi - ca - bo Ec - cle - si-
et su - per hanc pe-tram ae - di - fi-ca - - bo, ae - di - fi - ca - bo,
tram, et su - per hanc pe - tram ae - di - fi - ca - bo Ec - cle - si - am me -
tram ae - di - fi - ca - bo, ae- di - fi - ca-bo Ec - cle - si-am me - am, Ec-
tram ae - di - fi - ca - bo

90
bo Ec - cle - si - am me - am, Ec - cle - si - am me -
am, Ec - cle - si - am, Ec - cle - si - am, Ec - cle - si - am, Ec - cle - si-
ae - di - fi - ca - bo, ae - di - fi - ca - bo Ec-
am, Ec - cle - si - am me - am, Ec - cle - si - am me -
cle - si - am me - am, Ec - cle - si - am me - am, Ec - cle - si - am,
Ec - cle - si - am me - am, Ec - cle - si - am me - am,
95
100
am, Ec - cle - si - am me - am.
am me - am, Ec - cle - si - am me - am, Ec - cle - si - am me - am.
cle - si - am me - am, Ec - cle - si - am, Ec - cle - si - am me - am.
am, Ec - cle - si - am me - am.
Ec - cle - si - am, Ec - cle - si - am me - am.
Ec - cle - si - am me - am, Ec - cle - si - am me - am.
SECUNDA PARS
105
Pe - tre, di - li - gis, Pe - tre di - li - gis me? Qui re - spon-
Pe - tre, di - li - gis, di - li - gis me? Qui
Pe - tre, di - li - gis me, di - li - gis me? Qui re - spon - dens, qui
Pe - tre, di - li - gis me? Qui re - spon-
Pe - tre, di - li - gis, di - li - gis me?
Pe - tre, Pe - tre, di - li - gis me?

110
dens a - it, qui re-spon-dens, a - -
re-spon dens a - it, qui re-spon-dens a - it, a - it: Tu
re-spon-dens, qui re-spon-dens a - -
dens a - it, qui re-spon-dens a - -
Qui re-spon-dens a - it:
Qui re-spon-dens a - it, a -
115
it: Tu scis, Do - - mi - ne, tu scis, Do-
scis, Do - - mi - ne, tu scis, Do - mi - ne, Do -
it: Tu scis, Do - - mi - ne,
it: Tu scis, Do - - mi - ne, tu scis, Do - - -
Tu scis, Do - - mi - ne, tu scis, Do - mi -
it: Tu scis, Do - -
120
- mi - ne, qui - a a - mo te
- mi - ne, qui - a a - mo te et a - ni-mam me -
qui - a a - mo te, qui - a a - mo te, qui - a a - mo te
- mi - ne, qui - a a - mo te, a - mo te et a -
ne, qui - a a - mo te, a - mo te, a - mo te et a -
- mi - ne qui - a a - mo te, qui - a a - mo te et

125
130
et a - ni-mam me - am po - no pro te, po -
am po - no pro te. Et
et a - ni-mam me-am po - no pro te. Et a - it Ie -
- ni-mam me-am po - no pro te, po - no pro te.
- ni-mam me- am po - no pro te, po - - no pro
a - ni - mam me-am po-no pro
135
no pro te. Et a - it Ie - sus: Pa - sce o - ves me as, pa-
a - it Ie - sus, et a - it Ie-sus, et a - it Ie - sus: Pa-
- sus, et a - it Ie - sus: Pa - sce o - ves me - as, pa-
Et a - it Ie - - sus, et a - it Ie - sus:
te. Et a - it Ie - sus: Pa-sce o - ves me - as,
te. Et a - it Ie - sus: Pa-sce o -
140
- sce o - ves me-as, pa- sce o - ves me - as, pa - sce o-ves me - as.
sce o - ves me - as, pa-sce o-ves me - as. E - go e - nim pro te ro-
sce o - ves me - as, pa - sce o - ves me - as. E - go e - nim pro te ro - ga -
Pa - sce o - ves me - as, pa - sce o - ves me - as. E - go e -
pa - sce o - ves me - as, o - ves me - as. E -
ves me - as, pa - sce o - ves me - as.

145
E - go e - nim pro te ro-ga - - vi ut non de - fi - ci -
ga - - vi, e - go e - nim pro te ro - ga -
- vi, e - go e - nim pro te ro - ga - vi
nim pro te ro - ga - vi, pro te ro - ga - vi, pro te ro - ga -
go e - nim pro te ro - ga - vi, e - go e - nim pro te ro - ga - vi, te ro - ga -
E - go e - nim pro te ro - ga - - vi, ro - ga -
150
at, ut non de - fi - ci - at fi -
vi, pro te ro - ga - vi ut non de - fi - ci - at fi - des tu -
ut non de - fi - ci - at, ut non de - fi - ci - at fi - des tu - -
vi ut non de - fi - ci - at fi - des tu - a, fi - des tu - a, ut non de - fi - ci -
vi ut non de - fi - ci - at, ut non de - fi - ci - at fi - des tu - a,
vi ut non de - fi - ci - at fi - des tu - -
155
160
des tu - a, tu - a et tu a - li - quan - do con - ver - sus, a - li -
a, fi - des tu - - a et tu
- a, fi - des tu - a et tu a - lin - quan - do
at fi - des tu - a, tu - a et tu a - li quan - do con - ver - sus,
fi - des tu - a et tu a - li - quan -
a et tu a - li - quan - do

165
quan- do con- ver - sus con - fir - ma fra - tres tu - os, con - fir -
a - li - quan - do con - ver - sus con - fir - ma fra - tres tu - -
con - ver - sus con - fir - ma fra - tres tu - os, con -
con - ver - - sus con - fir - ma fra - tres tu -
do con - ver - sus con - fir - ma fra - tres tu - os,
con - ver - sus con - fir - ma fra - tres tu -
170
ma fra - tres tu - os. Al - le - lu - ia, al - le - lu - ia, al -
os. Al - le - lu - ia, al - le - lu - ia, al - le -
fir - ma fra - tres tu - os. Al - le - lu - ia, al - le - lu - ia, al - le - lu - ia,
- os. Al - le - lu - ia, al - le - lu - ia, al - le - lu - ia, al -
con - fir - ma fra - tres tu - os. Al - le - lu - ia, al - le - lu - ia, al -
os. Al - le - lu - ia, al - le - lu - ia,
175
le - lu - ia, al - le - lu - ia, al - le - lu - ia, al - le - lu - ia.
lu - ia, al - le - lu - ia, al - le - lu - ia.
al - le - lu - ia, al - le - lu - ia, al - le - lu - ia, al - le - lu - ia.
le - lu - ia, al - le - lu - ia, al - le - lu - ia, al - le - lu - ia.
le - lu - ia, al - le - lu - ia, al - le - lu - ia, al - le - lu - ia, al - le - lu - ia.
al - le - lu - ia, al - le - lu - ia, al - le - lu - ia.

62 CRISTÓBAL DE MORALES *Missa Quaeramus cum pastoribus:* Kyrie

Cristobal de Morales, *Opera Omnia*. Vol. 1. Ed. Angles. In *Monumentos de la Música Española* 9 (Barcelona: Consejo Superior de Investigaciones Científicas, 1952), 148–54.

15
e - le - i - son, Ky - ri - e
- ri - e e - le - -
Ky - ri - e e - lei - son, Ky -
son, Ky - ri - e, Ky - ri -
e - le - i - son, Ky - ri - e e - le - i -
20
e - le - i - son, Ky - ri - e
i - son, Ky - ri - e e -
ri - e, Ky - ri - e e - lei - son, Ky -
e e - lei - son, Ky - ri - e e - lei -
son, Ky - ri - e e - le - i - son,
25
e - le - i - son, e - le - i - son,
le - i - son, Ky - ri - e e - le - i -
ri - e e - le - - i - son, Ky -
son, Ky - ri - e e - le - i - son,
Ky - ri - e e - lei - son, Ky - ri - e e - lei -

30
Ky - ri - e e - le - i -
son, Ky - ri - e e - le - i - son, Ky - ri - e
ri - e e - le - i - son, Ky - ri - e e - le - i
Ky - ri - e e - le - i - son, Ky - ri - e e - le - i -
son, e - le - i - son,
35
Ky - ri - e e - le - i - son.
e - le - i - son, Ky - ri - e - e - le - i - son.
son, Ky - ri - e e - le - i - son.
son, Ky - ri - e e - le - i - son.
Ky - ri - e e - lei - son.
40
Chri - ste e - le - i - son,
Chri - ste e - le -
Chri - ste e - le -

45
Chri - ste e - le - - -
Chri - ste e - le - -
Chri - ste e - le -
- i - son, Chri -
- - - - i - son,
50
- - i - son, Chri - ste e - le - i -
- - - - i - son, Chri -
- - i - son, Chri - ste e - le - i - son,
ste e - le - i - son, Chri - ste e -
Chri - ste e - le - i -
55
son, Christe e - le - i - son, e -
ste e - le - i - son, Chri - ste e - le - i - son,
e - le - i - son, Chri - ste
le - i - son, Chri -
son, Chri - ste,

60
le - i - son, Chri - ste e - le - - - i -
Chri - ste e - le - -
e - le - i - son, Chri - ste e - le -
ste e - le - i - son, Chri - ste e - le - i - son,
e - le - i - son, Chri - ste e - le - i -
65
son, Chri - ste e - le - i - son.
- i - son, Chri - ste e - lei - son.
- i - son, Chri-ste e - le - i - son.
Chri - ste e - le - i - son, Chri-ste e - le - i - son.
son, Chri - ste e - le - i - son.
70
Ky - ri - e e - le - i -
Ky - ri - e e - le - - - i -
Ky - ri - e e - le - i - son, Ky - ri -
Ky - ri - e e - le - i - son,
Ky - ri - e e - le - i - son, Ky - ri - e e - le -

75
son, Ky - ri - e e - le - i - son,
son, e - le - i - son, Ky - ri - e
e e - le - - - i - son,
Ky - ri - e e - le - i - son, e -
- - i - son, Ky - ri -
80
85
Ky - ri - e e - le - i - son,
e - le - i - son, e - le - i - son, Ky -
Ky - ri - e e - le - i - son, Ky -
- le - i - son, Ky - ri - e
e e - le - - i - son, Ky - ri - e e - le -
90
Ky - ri - e e - le - -
- ri - e e - le - - -
ri - e e - le - - - -
e - le - i - son, Ky - ri - e
- i - son, Ky - ri - e e - le - i - son,

95
- i - son, Ky - ri - e e -
- - i - son, Ky - ri - e
- i - son, Ky - ri - e, Ky - ri - e
e - le - i - son,
Ky - ri - e, Ky - ri - e e - le - i - son,
100
le - i - son, e - le - i - son, Ky - ri - e
e - le - - - - i -
e - le - - i - son, Ky - ri -
Ky - ri - e e - le - i -
Ky - ri - e e - lei -
105
Ky - ri - e e - le - i - son.
son, Ky - ri - e e - le - i - son.
e e - le - i - son.
son, Ky - ri - e e - lei - son, Ky - ri - e e - lei - son.
son, Ky - ri - e e - le - i - son.

63 CLAUDIN DE SERMISY *Je n'ay point plus d'affection*

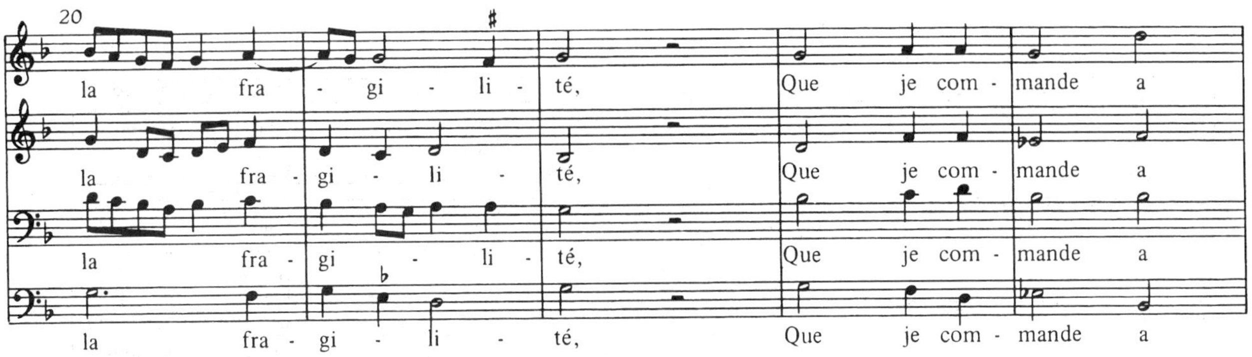
20
la fra - gi - li - té, Que je com - mande a
la fra - gi - li - té, Que je com - mande a
la fra - gi - li - té, Que je com - mande a
la fra - gi - li - té, Que je com - mande a

25
mon vou-loir, Rien n'y peult la fra - gi - li - té.
mon vou-loir, Rien n'y peult la fra - gi - li - té.
mon vou-loir, Rien n'y peult la fra - gi - li - té.
mon vou-loir, Rien n'y peult la fra - gi - li - té,

64 PIERRE PASSEREAU *Il est bel et bon*

20
Il est bel et bon, bon, bon, bon, bon, com - mè - re, com-mè - re, com-mè - re, mon ma -
mè - re; Il est bel et bon, bon, bon, com - mè - re, com-mè - re, mon ma -
re, Il est bel et bon, bon, bon, com - mè - re, com - mè - re, mon ma -
mè - re; Il est bel et bon, bon, bon, com - mè - re, mon ma -
25
ry. Il ne me cou - rou - ce ne me bat aus - si;
ry. Il ne me cou - rous - se ne me bat aus - sy;
ry. Il ne me cou - rous - se
ry. Il ne me cou -
30
Il faict le mes - na - ge, Il donne aux pou - lail - les
Il faict le mes - na - ge, Il donne
ne me bat aus - si Il faict le mes - na - ge Il donne aux pou -
rous - se ne me bat aus - sy Il faict le mes - na - ge
35
Il donne aux pou - lail - les Et je prens mes plai - sirs. Com - mè -
aux pou - lail - les Et je prens mes plai - sirs.
lail - les Et je prens mes plai - sirs. Com -
Il donne aux pou - lail - les Et je prens mes plai - sirs.
40
- re, c'est pour ri - re Quant les pou - lail - les cri -
Com - mè - re, c'est pour ri - re Quant les pou -
mère, est ce pour ri - re Quant les pou - lail - les
Com - mère, est ce pour ri - re Quant les

45
50
55
ent Quant les pou - lail - les cri - ent Pe - ti - te co-
lail les cri - ent Co co co co co co co
cri - ent Quant les pou - lail - les cri - ent Pe -
pour lail - les cri - ent Co co co co co dac, co co
que - te, pe - ti - te co- que - te, pe - ti - te co- que - te, pe - ti - te co -
co co co co dac, co co co co co co co co dac, co co co co dac, co
ti - te co - quet - te, pe - ti - te co - que - te, pe - ti - te co - que - te, pe -
dac, co co dac, co co co dac, co co co co co co dac, co co dac, pe -
que - te qu'es - se cy? Il est bel et bon, bon,
co dac, mon a - my qu'es - se cy?
ti - te co - que - te qu'es - se cy? Il est bel et
ti - te co - que - te qu'es - se cy?
bon, bon, bon, com - mè - re Il est bel et bon, bon,
Il est bel et bon, bon, bon, bon, bon, com - mè - re;
bon, bon, bon, bon, bon, com - mè - re; Il est bel et
Il est bel et bon, bon, bon, com - mè - re;
bon, bon, bon, com - mè - re, com - mè - re, com- mè - re, mon ma - ry.
Il est bel et bon, bon, bon, com - mè - re, com- mè - re, mon ma - ry.
bon, bon, bon, com - mè - re, com - mè - re, mon ma - ry.
Il est bel et bon, bon, bon, com - mè - re, mon ma - ry.

65 CLÉMENT JANEQUIN *Les cris de Paris*

20
Les cris de Pa - ris
Les cris de Pa -
vou - - lez ou - yr, ou - - yr
les
ris
les cris de Pa - ris
Les cris de Pa - ris
25
cris, les cris de Pa - -
les cris de Pa - ris,
les cris de Pa -
les cris de Pa - ris,
30
ris, les cris de Pa - ris,
les cris de Pa - ris, les
ris, les cris de Pa - ris,
les cris de Pa - ris,
35
de Pa - ris?
cris de Pa - - ris?
de Pa - ris?
les cris de Pa - ris?

Pas - tez tres tous chaulx, tous
Ou sont ilz ces pe-tiz pi-ons, ou sont ilz
chaulx, qui l'ai-ra, lai-ra, qui l'ai-ra, l'ai-ra
ces pe-tiz pi-ons? Vin blanc, vin cle-ret, vin ver-meil, a six de -
Je les don-ne,
niers, a six de -
Tar - - te - let - tes fri - an - -
Cas - se mu - seaux tous chaulx
je les vendz, je les don - ne, je les vendz.
niers. Et est a l'en-sei - gne du ber -
des a la bel - le gauf - fre, a la bel - le
je don - ne, je les vendz, je les
sa a boy - re, sa, sa a boy - re, ca.
seau qui est en la ru - e de la Har - pe.
gauf - fre, a la bel - le gauf - fre.
vendz, je les don - ne pour ung pe - tit blanc.

Ai - gre, vin ai - gre, ai - gre, vin ai - gre.
Ha - renc de la nuyt, ha - renc de la nuyt, ha - renc
Fault il point de sault - -
Mou - star - - - - -
Ha - renc blanc, ha - renc blanc, ha - renc de la nuyt, ha - renc
blanc, ha - renc blanc, ha - renc. Mou - star - de,
- - ce vert, fault il point de
de, mou - star - -
55
de la nuyt, ha - renc de la nuyt. Co - trez
mou - star - de fi - - ne. Sou - liers
saul - - ce vert?
de, mou - star - - de mou -
secz, co - trez.
vieux, sou - liers vieux. Choux ge - lez, choux ge -
Ar - de bu - - che, ar - de bu - - che,
star - - - de.
60
Choux ge - lez, choux ge - lez choux
lez, choux ge - lez, choux ge - lez,
bu - - che. Choux ge -
Hault et bas ra - mon -

ge - lez, choux ge - lez. Ar - de
choux ge - lez
lez, choux ge - lez choux ge - lez,
nez les ca - mi - na - - - des.
65
bu - che, bu - - che. Qui veult
choux ge-lez, ge - lez.
choux ge-lez, choux ge - lez. Qui
Choux ge-lez, choux ge - lez.
du laict, qui veult du laict? Poys vers, poys
Qui veult du laict qui veult du
veult du laict? Poys vers, poys vers, poys vert.
C'est moy, c'est moy, je meurs de froit.
70
vers. Mes bel - les les -
laict, qui veult du laict? Mes bel - les les - tues mes
Mes bel - les les - tues, mes beaulx ci - botz,
Mes bel-les les-tues, mes beaulx ci - botz,

tues, mes beaulx ci - botz
beaulx ci - botz mes beaulx ci - botz, mes
mes bel - les les - tues, mes beaulx ci -
mes beaulx ci - botz, mes bel - les les - tues, mes
mes bel - les les - tues, mes beaulx ci - botz.
bel - les les - tues, mes beaulx ci - botz, beaulx ci - botz.
botz mes bel - les les - tues, mes beaulx ci -
beaulx ci - botz, mes bel - les les - tues, mes beaulx ci -
Fault il point de
Gui-gne, doul-ce gui - gne. Fault il point
botz. Fault il
botz. Gui-gne, doul-ce gui - gne.
sa - blon? Ar -
de sa - blon? Ar - gent m'y duit, ar - gent m'y
point de sa - blon?
Voir - re jo - ly, voi - re jo - ly.
gent m'y fault, ar - gent m'y duit ar - gent m'y duit.
duit. Gai - gne pe - tit, gai - gne pe - tit.
Ar - gent m'y fault, ar - gent m'y fault, ar - gent m'y
Lye, ly - - - - -

A - lu - met, a - lu - met, a - lu -
Ar - gent m'y fault, ar - gent m'y fault.
fault. A - lu - met, a - lu -
- - - - - e.
90
met, a - lu - met, a - lu - met a - lu - met.
A - lu - met, a - lu - met, a - lu - met
met, a - lu - met a - lu -
Hou - seaux vieux, hou - seaux vieux.
Pru - neaux de Saint Ju - li - en, pru - neaux de Saint Ju - li - en.
a - lu - met, a - lu - met, a - lu - met.
met, a - lu - met, a - lu - met.
Feb - ves de Ma - retz, feb - - ves.
95
Je fais le co - qu, moy, je fais le co - qu,
Je fais le co - qu, moy, je fais le co - qu, moy,
Je fais le co - qu, moy, je fais le co - qu,
moy. Ma bel - le po - rée, mon beau per - sin, ma
Ma bel - le po - ré - e, mon beau per - sin, mes beaulx es - pi -
moy.
moy.

100
belle o - seil - le, mes beaulx es - pi - nards.
nards, ma belle o - seil - - - -
O - renge, o - ren - ge.
le. Pe-ches de Cor-beil, pe-ches
Pe-ches de Cor-beil, pe-ches de Cor-beil, pe-ches de Cor-
Pe-ches de Cor-beil, pe-ches de Cor-beil, pe-ches
105
de Cor-beil, pe - ches de Cor - beil.
beil, pe-ches de Cor - - beil, pe - -
de Cor-beil, pe-ches de Cor - beil.
Pi-gnes vui-dez, pi-gnes vui-dez pi-gnes vui-dez,
Pi-gnes vui-dez, pi-gnes vui-dez
- - ches de Cor - beil. Pi-gnes vui-dez,
Pi-gnes vui-dez, pi-gnes vui-dez, pi-gnes vui-dez,
pi-gnes vui-dez. Char-lo -
pi-gnes vui-dez. Char-lo - te m'a -
pi-gnes vui-dez, pi-gnes vui-dez.
pi-gnes vui-dez, pi-gnes vui-dez. Char-lo - te m'a

110
te m'a - my - e. A - pe - tit, a - pe - tit nou - veau, a - pe -
my - e, Char - lo - te m'a - my - e. A - pe - tit nou - veau, a - pe -
Char - lo - te m'a - my - e. A - pe - tit nou - veau, a - pe -
my - e A - pe - tit nou - veau, a - pe -
tit nou - veau pe - tit, a - pe - tit nou - veau, a - pe - tit nou -
tit nou - veau pe - tit, a - pe - tit nou - veau, a - pe - tit nou -
tit nou - veau pe - tiz, a - pe - tit nou - veau.
tit nou - veau pe - tit, a - pe - tit nou - veau.
115
veau. A - men - dez vous da - mes, a - men -
veau. A - men - dez vous da - mes, a - men -
A - men - dez vous da - mes, a - men - dez,
A - men - dez vous da - mes, a - men - dez,
dez. A - le - man - de nou - vel - le,
dez. A - le - man - de nou - vel - le,
a - men - dez vous da - mes, a - men - dez.
a - men - dez vous da - mes, a - men - dez.
a - le - man - de nou - vel - le a - le -
a - le - man - de nou - vel - le a - le -
A - le - man - de nou - vel - le, a - le -
A - le - man - de nou - vel - le, a - le -

man - de nou-vel - - - le.
man - de nou-vel - - le. Na - vetz, na - vetz, na-vetz,
man - de nou-vel - - - le.
man - de nou-vel - - - le. Na -
Na - vetz, na - vetz, na - vetz, na -
na - vetz na - vetz, na -
Na - vetz na - vetz, na-vetz, na - vetz na-vetz, na -
vetz, na - vetz, na - - vetz, na - vetz na-vetz, na -
Ra - ve doul - ce, ra - ve
Ra - ve doul - ce, ra - ve.
Ra - ve doul - ce, ra - ve, ra - ve doul - ce,
Feu - re, feu - re Bri - .
ra - ve doul - ce ra - ve, ra - ve. A ung tour -
A ung tour - noys le cha - pel - let, a ung tour -
ra - ve. A ung tour - noys le cha - pel -
- e, Bri - - e.

135
noys le cha - pe - let, a ung tour - noys le cha - pel -
noys le cha - pel - let. Cher - vis,
let, a ung tour - noys le cha - pel - let. Cher -
Mar - rons de Ly - on, mar - rons de Ly -
140
let. Mes beaulx pe - sons,
cher - vis, cher- vis. Mes beaulx pe - sons, mes
vis, cher - vis, cher - vis, cher-vis, cher - vis.
on, mar - rons de Ly - on, mar - rons de Ly -
mes beaulx pe-sons. A - lu-met, a - lu - met, a - lu-met-tes seches,
beaulx pe - sons. Vin nouveau, vin nou- veau, vin nouveau.
A - lu - met, a - lu-met, a - lu-met, a - lu-met-tes seches, a - lu -
on, de Ly-on. A mes beaulx pe-sons.
145
a - lu - met, a - lu - met, a - lu - met.
A - lu - met, a - lu -
met, a - lu - met.
A - lu - met, a - lu - met - tes

Fault il point de
met - tes se - ches, a - lu - met. Fault il
Fault il point de grois,
se - ches, a - lu - met.
grois, fault il point de grois?
point de grois, fault il point de
fault il point de
150
grois, fault il point de grois, fault il point de grois? Choux, choux
grois, fault il point de grois, fault il point de grois? Pe - tiz
Fault il point de boys, fault il point de boys, fault il
155
Choux, choux, pe - tiz choux,
choux tous chaulx, choux tous chaulx, choux tous chaulx.
choux tous chaulx, pe - tit choux tous chaulx.
point de gros boys? Choux ge - lez.
pe - tiz choux. Et qui l'au-ra le
Et qui l'au-ra le mou-le de gros boys
Et qui l'au-ra le
Et qui l'au-ra le mou-le de gros boys

160
mou-le de gros boys, le mou-le de gros boys?
le mou - le de gros boys?
mou-le de gros boys, de gros boys?
le mou - le de gros boys?
Es - chaudez chaux, eschaudez chaux.
Es - chaudez chaux, eschaudez chaux, eschaudez chaux, eschaudez chaux.
Es - chaudez
Es - chaudez
165
Se - che bour - rée, se -
Se - che bour - ré -
chaux, es - chau - dez chaux.
chaux, es - chau - dez chaux, es - chau - dez chaux, es - chau - dez chaux.
- che bour - rée, se-che bour-ré - - e.
e, se-che bour-ré - - e, se che bour-ré -
Se-che bour - ré - e,
Se-che bour-ré -
170
e, se - che bour - ré - - - -
se - che bour - ré - e, bour - ré - - -
e, se - che bour - ré - e, se - che bour-ré - -

Ser-ceau, ser-ceau, beau ser-ceau, ser - ceau
e. Ser-teau, ser-teau, beau ser-teau, ser -
e. Ser-ceau, beau ser-ceau, ser - ceau,
e. Ser-teau, ser-teau, beau ser-teau
175
serceau, serceau, beau ser - ceau. Ar - de chan -
teau. Ar - de chandel - le, ar - -
serceau, serceau, beau ser - ceau, ser - ceau.
serteau, serteau, beau ser - teau, ser - teau.
180
delle, ar - de chan - del - le.
de chan - del - - le.
Ar - de chan - delle, ar - de chan -
Ar - de chandelle, ar -
Fa - lour - de, fa - lour-de, fa - lour-de,
Fa - lour - de, fa - lour-de, fa -
del - - le.
- de chandel - le. Fa - lour - -
185
fa - lour - - de.
- - lour - de.
Fa - lourde, fa - lourde fa-lourde, fa - -
de, fa - lour - de fa - lourde, fa - lourde, fa -

190
A Pa - ris sur pe - - tit pont
A Pa - ris sur pe - tit
- - - lour - de.
- - lour - de.
ge - li - - ne de feur - - - re.
pont ge - li - ne de feur - re.
A
A Pa - ris sur pe - tit
195
Pa - ris sur pe - tit pont ge - li - - ne de
pont, a Pa - ris sur pe - tit pont ge - li - ne de
200
A Pa - ris sur pe - tit pont ge - li - ne de
A Pa-ris sur pe - tit pont ge - li -
feur - re ge - li - ne de
feur - - re ge - li - ne de
205
feur - re. Si vous en vou - lez plus ou -
ne de feur - re. Si vous en vou - lez plus ou - yr
feur - - re.
feur - - re. Si vous en vou - lez plus ou -

210
yr al - lez al - lez, al - lez al - lez, al -
al - lez al - lez, al - lez al - lez, al - lez,
Al - lez, al - lez, al - lez al - lez, al -
yr al - lez, al - lez, al - lez al - lez, al -
lez, al - lez les donc quer -
al - lez les donc quer - - - -
lez, al - lez, al - lez.
lez, al - lez les donc
215
- - re al -
- - re al -
Si vous en vou - lez plus ou - yr al - lez
si vous en vou - lez plus ou - yr al -
220
lez al - lez, al - lez al - lez, al - lez
lez al - lez, al - lez al - lez, al - lez
al - lez, al - lez, al - lez les donc · al -
lez al - lez, al - lez al - lez, al - lez

225
al - lez, al - lez si
al - lez, al - lez si vous en
lez, al - lez les donc quer - re
al - lez, al - lez les donc quer -
vous en vou - lez plus si vous en vou - lez
vou - lez plus ou - yr, si vous en vou - lez plus ou -
si vous en vou - lez
- - re si vous en vou - lez
230
plus ou-yr al - lez al - lez, al - lez al -
yr al - lez al - lez, al - lez al - lez, al -
plus ou-yr al - lez al - lez, al - lez al -
plus ou-yr al - lez al - lez, al - lez al -
235
lez les donc al - lez les donc quer - - re.
lez al - lez, al - lez les donc quer - - re.
lez, al - lez al - lez les donc quer - - re.
lez, al - lez al - lez les donc quer - - re.

66 PHILIPPE VERDELOT *Madonna, per voi ardo*

 Colin H. Slim, ed., *A Gift of Madrigals and Motets.* Vol. 2. Chicago: University of Chicago Press, 1972), pp. 353–55.

25
- te, Don - - na, non v'ac - cor - ge - te Che per voi mo - ro et
- te, Don - - na, non v'ac - cor - - ge - te Che per voi mo - ro et
- te, Don - - na, non v'ac - cor - ge - te
- te, Don - na, non v'ac - cor - ge - te
30
ar - do? Et per mi - rar vo - stra bel - tà in - fi - ni - ta
ar - do? Et per mi - rar vo - stra bel - tà in - fi - - ni - ta
Che per voi mo - ro et ar - do? Et per mi - - rar vo - stra bel - tà in - fi - - ni - ta
Che per voi mo - ro et ar - do? Et per mi - rar vo - stra bel - tà in - fi - ni - ta
35
Et voi so - la ser - vir bra - - - mo la vi - - ta,
Et voi so - la ser - vir bra - mo la vi - ta,
Et voi so - la ser - vir bra - mo la vi - ta,
Et voi so - la ser - vir bra - mo la vi - ta,
40
Et voi so - la ser - vir bra - - mo la vi - - ta.
Et voi so - la ser - vir bra - - mo la vi - ta.
Et voi so - la ser - vir bra - - mo la vi - ta.
Et voi so - la ser - vir bra - -mo la vi - ta.

67 JACQUES ARCADELT *Il bianco e dolce cigno*

a - - - - - to, mor - te che nel mo - ri - re,
ro be - a - - - - to, mor - te che nel mo - ri - re,
ro, et io mo - ro be - a - to, mor - te che nel mo - ri - re,
et io mo - ro be - a - - - to, mor - te che nel mo - ri - re,
m'em - pie di gio - ia tutt' e di de - si - re, se nel mo - rir'
m'em - pie di gio - ia tutt' e di de - si - re, se nel mo - rir'
m'em - pie di gio - ia tutt' e di de - si - re, se nel mo - rir'
m'em - pie di gio - ia tutt' e di de - si - re, se nel mo - rir'
al - tro do - lor non sen - to, di mil - le
al - tro do - lor non sen - to, di mil - le mort' il di, di mil - le
al - tro do - lor non sen - to, di mil - le mort' il di, di mil - le
al - tro do - lor non sen - to, di mil - le mort' il di,
mort' il dì sa - rei con - ten - to, di mil - le mort' il dì sa -
mort' il dì, di mil - le mort' il di, di mil - le mort' il dì,
mort' il dì sa - rei con - ten - to, di mil - le mort' il di, di mil - le mort' il dì sa -
sa - rei con - ten - to, di mil - le mort' il dì sa -
rei con - ten - to.
di mil - le mort' il dì sa - rei con - ten - - - - to.
rei con - ten - to, di mil - le mort' il di sa - rei con - ten - to.
rei con - ten - to, di mil - le mort' il dì, sa - rei con - ten - to.

68 LUDWIG SENFL *Das G'läut zu Speyer*

 Ludwig Senfl, *Sämtliche Werke*. Vol. 4. Ed. Geering and Altwegg (Basel: Kommissionsverlag Hug, 1940), pp. 109–112.

gling. Laßt mehr an - gehn, da müeßt ihr zue mir her stehn. Gling
mich, sunst hör' auf ich. Flux, fu - der dich. Gling, glang, gling, glang,
nicht klagt' an, noch nicht flieht, ziecht an, ziecht, streckt die Arm', macht euch warm. Gling, glang,
daß Glock'schall'. Mar, mir, mur, maun, mar, mer, mir, mur, maun, mar, mer, mir,
läu - ten wöl - len. Mir, mur, maun. Nu zue die - sem Fest
mur, maun, bum, mur, maun, bum, mur, maun, bum,
glang, gling, glang, gling, glang, gling, glang, gling, glang, gling, glang, gling,
gling, glang, gling, glang, gling, glang, gling, glang. Ich mag nicht läu-ten lang. Gling, glang,
gling, glang, gling, glang, gling, glang, gling, glang, gling, glang, gling, glang,
mur, maun, mar, mer, mir, mur, maun, mar, mer, mir, mur, maun, mir, mur, maun. Streck' an, streck'
tuet all-sambt das Best', nehmt hin Strick' und Seil', ziecht an resch mit Eil'. Mur, maun, mur,
mur, maun, bum, mur, maun, bum, mur, maun, bum, mar, mur, maun,
glang, gling, glang, gling, glang. Mit un-sern Glocken laßt zammen
gling, glang, gling, glang. Bitt' ich, mir sag', was ist für Tag,
gling, glang, gling, glang, gling, glang. So Hans und Paul, ziecht,
an, was ein je der mit der Macht kann. Mar, mer, mir, maun,
maun, mur, maun, mur, maun. So tuet zamm-stehn, last's wohl auf
bum, mar, mir, mur, maun, bum, mer, mur, maun, bum, mir, mur, maun, bum,

40
lok-ken, ziecht un-er-schrok-ken. Gling, glang, gling, glang, gling, glang,
was hab' wir heut', daß man so läut'. Gling, glang,
seid nit faul. Wie schnauft ihr mit dem Maul? Gling, glang,
mar, mer, mur, maun, mar, mer, mur, maun, gling, glang, gling,
geh'n, daß so viel zwen. Gling, glang, gling, glang. Jans, auch
mir, mur, maun, bum, mar, mir, mur, maun, bum, mur,
45
gling, glang, gling, glang, gling. Wie-wohl zwar An-dacht
gling, glang, gling, glang. Solch's Gläut macht mich be-tör'n, ich mag mich
gling, glang, bum. Nit ziecht so schnell, so klingt's baß
glang, gling. Seht zue mit und klenkt mit.
an-fang's. Jetzt klingt's wohl und geht ganz recht. So, so, mein Knecht.
maun, bum, mir, mur, maun, bum, mir, mur, maun, bum,
50 55
bloß, Gott's-dienst ist groß, geht ü-ber 's Gläut' am Kirchtag heut'. Gling, glang,
selbst nit hörn. Schau' e-ben auf, zeuch gleich mit auf. Gling, glang,
hell. So fein greift drein. Gling, glang,
Mur, maun, mur, maun, mur, maun. Gling, glang, gling,
Mur, maun, mar, maun. Hui, nun läut't zu-samm
mur, maun, mur, maun, mur, maun, bum, mur,

60
gling, glang, gling, glang, gling, glang, gling, glang, gling, glang, gling, gling,
gling, glang, gling, glang, gling, glang,
gling, glang, gling, glang, mar, mir, maun, mar,
glang, gling, glang, gling, glang, gling, glang. So läut't guet Ding, daß's ta -
in Got - tes Nam'. Wer kumbt, der kumbt. Hans, tue dich mun - ter
mur, maun, bum, mar, mer, mir, mur, maun, bum,
65
glang, gling, gling, glang, gling, gling, glang, gling. Die Schu - ler kom-men
gling, glang, gling, glang, gling, glang. Nun läut't zam in Got-tes Nam'.
mir, maun, mar, mir, maun, mar, mir, maun, bum. Nun läut't zammen in
- pfer kling', Maus, her an Ring, das O - pfer bring', weil man das Amt singt. Mar, mer,
umb, daß Glock' ent-brumm und schau' mit zue, daß's Seil nit brechen tue. Mur,
mir, mar, maun, bum, mir, mur, maun, bum, mir, mur, maun, bum, bum,
70
schon, Glocken brum- men, habt viel Sin - gens, gilt An-brin - gens, so Pfarrer auf- steht, gen O - pfer geht.
Wer kommen will, darf G'läuts nit viel, mag her tre - ten un - ge - be - ten zue der Met - ten.
Gott's Na-men. Wer will kum-men, hat's ver-num-men. An dem Fest heut' hab' wir lang gläut't. Mur, maun.
mir, mur, mar, mer, maun, mur, mar, mer, mir, maun, mar, mer, mir, maun, mar, mer, mir, maun, mir, mur, maun.
maun, mur, maun, mur, maun, mur, maun, mur, maun, mur, maun.
bum, bum, bum, bum, bum, bum.

Parisian Chanson

69a CLAUDIN DE SERMISY *Tant que vivray*

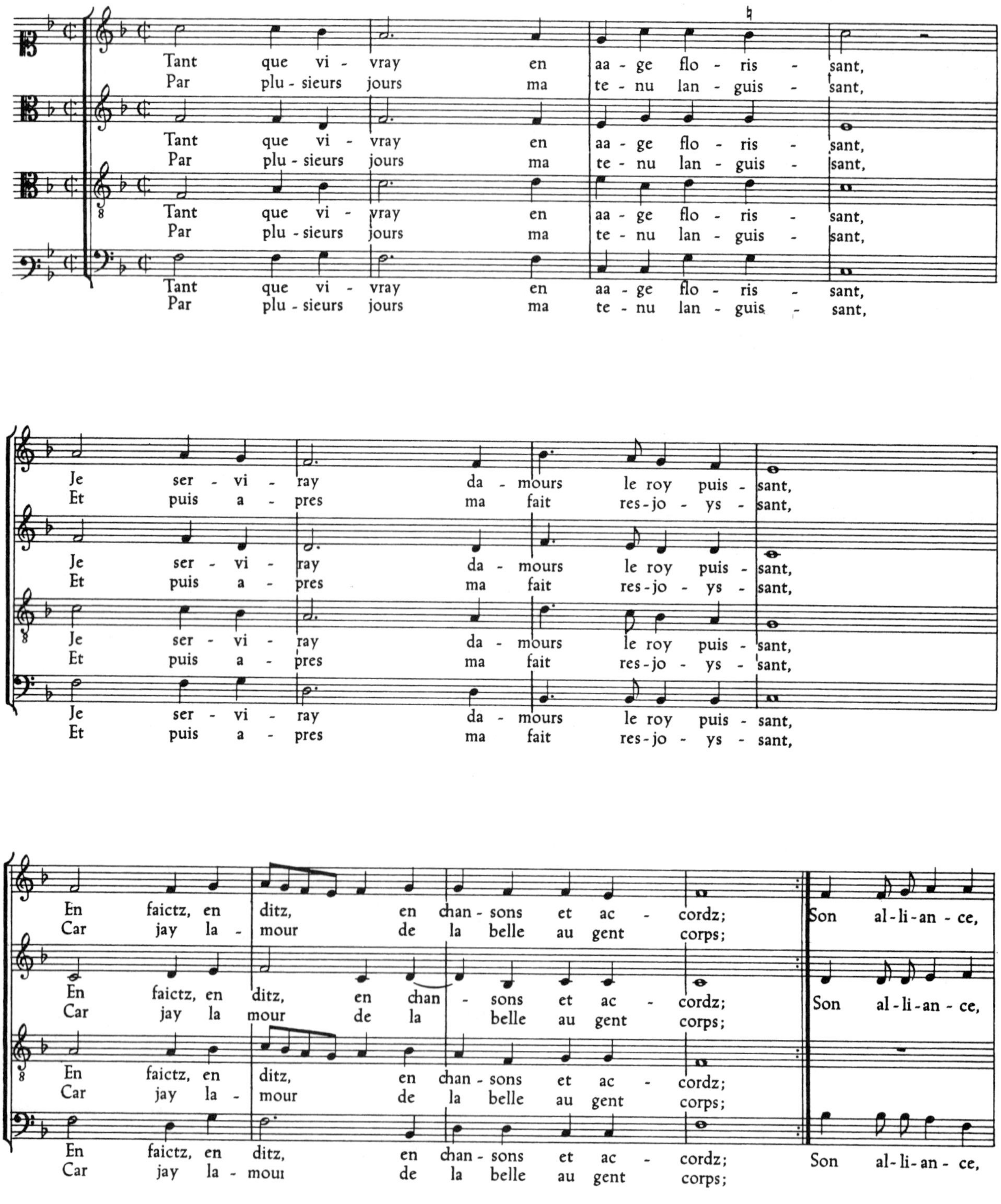

  Pierre Attaingnant, *Transcriptions for Keyboard*. Ed. Seay. In Corpus Mensurabilis Musicae 20, pp. 99–101.

Strophic form

Quand je la veulx servir et honnorer,
Quand par escriptz veulx son nom decorer,
Quand je la voy et visite souvent,
Les Envieulx n'en font que murmurer,
Mais nostre Amour n'en sçauroit moins durer,
Aultant ou plus en emporte le vent.
Maulgré envie
Toute ma vie
Je l'aymeray
Et chanteray;
C'est la premiere,
C'est la derniere,
Que j'ay servie et serviray.

69b IHAN GERO *Tant que vivray*

24
- le au corps gent. Son a - li - an - ce C'est ma fi - an -
la bel - le au corps gent. Son a - li - an - ce C'est ma fi -
27
- ce: Son cueur est mien; Le mien est sien. Fi de tris - tes -
- an - ce: Son cueur est mien; Le mien est sien. Fi de tris -
30
- se! Vi - ve li - es - se! Puis - qu'en a - mour (Puis - qu'en a - mour)
- tes - se! Vi - ve li - es - se! Puis - qu'en a - mour (Puis - qu'en a -
33
J'ay tant de bien.
- mour) J'ay tant de bien.

70 GIROLAMO CAVAZZONI *Christe redemptor omnium*

71 LUYS DE NARVÁEZ *Cuatro diferencias sobre Guárdame las vacas*

Luys de Narváez, *Luys de Narváez: Los seys libros del Delphin*. Ed. Pujol. In *Monumentos de la Música Española* 3 (Barcelona: Consejo Superior de Investigaciones Científicas, 1945), pp. 85–87.

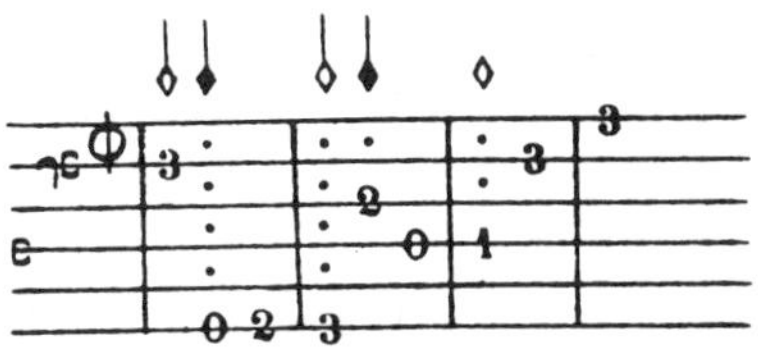

Tercera diferencia

Tercera diferencia

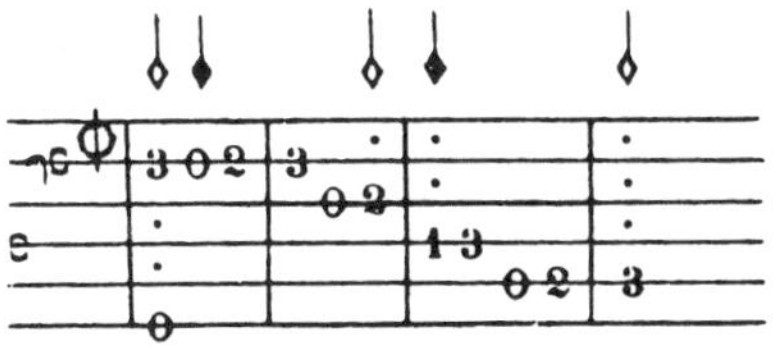

Quarta diferencia.

Cuarta diferencia.

72 ANTONIO DE CABEZÓN *Diferencias sobre las vacas*

Antonio de Cabezón, *The Collected Works of Antonio de Cabezón*. Vol. 1. Ed. Jacobs (Brooklyn: The Institute of Mediaeval Music, 1967), 76–79.

* Sharp not indicated in source. ** Rest indicated on first eighth note of soprano in source.

73 FRANCESCO CANOVA DA MILANO *Fantasia*

60
70
80
90
100

74 JULIO SEGNI DA MODENA *Ricercar*

 Colin H. Slim, ed., *Musica Nova.* In Monuments of Renaissance Music (Chicago: University of Chicago Press, 1964), pp. 21–25.

25
30
35
40

45
50
55
60

65
70
75
80

85

75 VINCENZO PELLEGRINI *Canzon detta la Serpentina*

30
35
40
3
2
45
C
50

55
60
65
3
2
70

c
75
80
85

76 CLAUDIO MERULO Toccata

Willi Apel and Archibald Davison, eds., *The Historical Anthology of Music.* Vol. 1. Rev. ed. (Cambridge, MA: Harvard University Press, 1977), pp. 168–70.

77 CLAUDE GERVAISE *Pavane d'Angleterre* and *Galliard*

GAILLARDE

 Johann Walter, *Sämtliche Werke*. Vol. 1. Ed. Schröder (Kassel: Bärenreiter, 1953), pp. 26–27. Used by kind permission of Bärenreiter-Verlag.

20
grau - sam Rü - stung ist; auf Erd ist nicht seins Glei - - - - chen.
List sein grau-sam Rü - stung ist; auf Erd ist nicht seins Glei - chen.
List sein grau - - sam Rü - stung ist; auf Erd ist nicht seins Glei - chen.
sein grau - sam Rü - stung ist; auf Erd ist nicht seins Glei - - chen.
sein grau-sam Rü - - stung ist; auf Erd ist nicht seins Glei - chen.
Rü - stung ist; auf Erd ist nicht seins Glei - - - - chen.

79 JACOBUS CLEMENS NON PAPA Two Psalm Settings from *Souterliedekens*

a. *Die boose sprack* (Psalm 36)

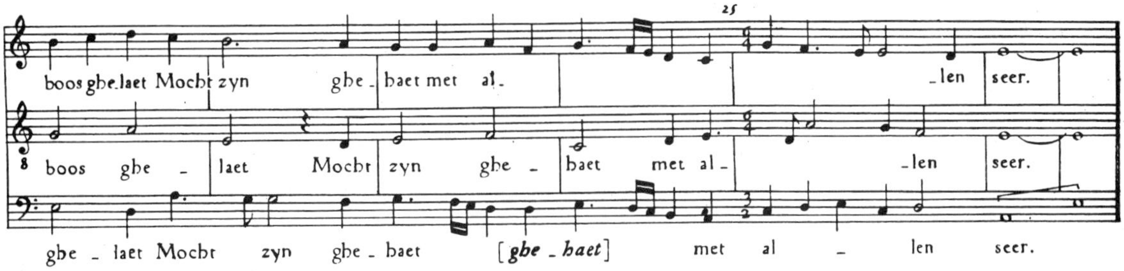
25
boos ghe.laet Mocht zyn ghe. baet met al. -len seer.
boos ghe - laet Mocht zyn ghe - baet met al - -len seer.
ghe - laet Mocht zyn ghe - baet [ghe - haet] met al - len seer.

b. *Vrolick en bly loeft God* (Psalm 66)

S
T (c.f.)
B
Vro - lick en bly loeft God ghi aert - sche sca -
Gheeft hem glo - ry syn lof wilt o - pen ba -
Vro - lick en bly loeft God ghi aert -
Gheeft hem glo - ry syn lof wilt o -
Vro - lick en bly loeft God ghi aert -
Gheeft hem glo - ry syn lof wilt o -

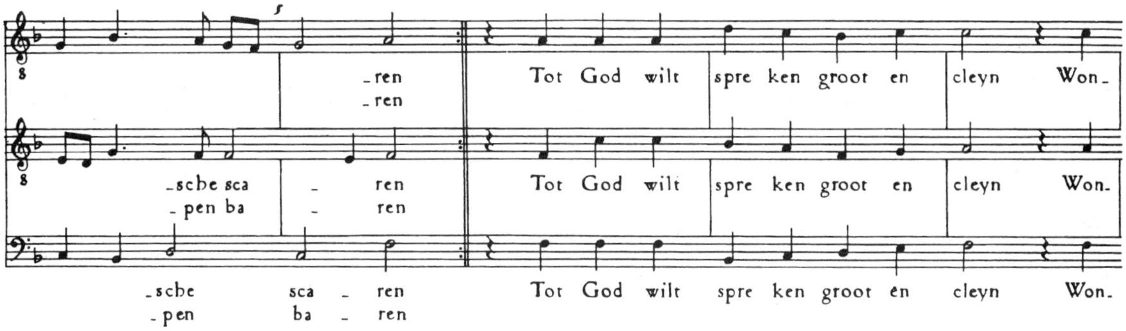
5
-ren Tot God wilt spre ken groot en cleyn Won -
-ren
-sche sca - ren Tot God wilt spre ken groot en cleyn Won.
-pen ba - ren
-sche sca - ren Tot God wilt spre ken groot en cleyn Won.
-pen ba - ren

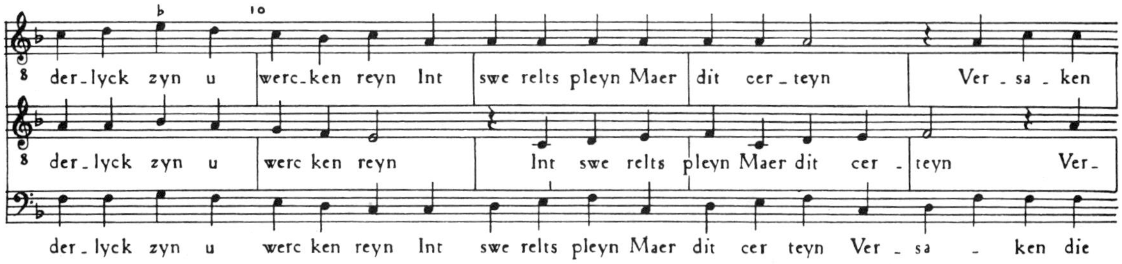
10
der-lyck zyn u werc-ken reyn Int swe relts pleyn Maer dit cer - teyn Ver - sa - ken
der - lyck zyn u werc ken reyn Int swe relts pleyn Maer dit cer - teyn Ver -
der - lyck zyn u werc ken reyn Int swe relts pleyn Maer dit cer teyn Ver - sa - ken die

15
die loe - ge na - -ren.
sa - ken die loe - -ge na - -ren.
loe ge na - -ren.

80 WILLIAM CORNYSH *Ah Robin, gentle Robin*

gen - tle Ro - bin tell me how thy le - man doth and thou shalt know of mine.
gen - tle Ro - bin tell me how thy le - man doth and thou shalt know of mine.
I find wo - men true; In faith my la - dy lov'th me well; She will change for no new.
25
Ah, Ro - bin, gen - tle Ro - bin, tell me how thy le - man doth and thou shalt know of mine.
Ah, Ro - bin, gen - tle Ro - bin, tell me how thy le - man doth and thou shalt know of mine.
Ah, Ro - bin, gen - tle Ro - bin, tell me how thy le - man doth and thou shalt know of mine.

81 JOHN TAVERNER *Western Wind* Mass: Sanctus

 Four- and Five-part Masses, ed. Hugh Benham. Early English Church Music, vol. 35.

20
Tr
M
C
B
San
25
ctus,
San
30
35
ctus,

40
Tr
M
C
B
Do - mi - nus
45
De
50
us
Sa - ba
55

60
Tr
M
C
B
oth;
oth;
oth;
oth;
65
ple
ple
ple
ni
70
ni
sunt coe
sunt coe
sunt coe
75
li et ter
li et ter
li et ter

Tr
C
M
B
80
85
90
95
100
105
ra
glo - ri - a
tu
a;

110
Tr
O – san – – – –
M
O – – – – – san –
C
O – – san – –
B
O – – - san – –
115
Tr
– – – – na in ex – –
M
– – – – na___ in ex – – –
C
– – – – na in ex –
B
– – – – na in ex – –
120
Tr
– – – – – – –
M
– – – – – – –
C
– – – cel – – – –
B
– – – – – – cel -
125
Tr
– – cel – – – – – –
M
– cel – – – – – –
C
– – – – – – –
B
– – – – – – –

Tr
M
C
B
130
sis;
sis;
sis;
sis;
135
be ne
be ne di
140
di
145
ctus
qui ve
ctus
qui ve
qui ve

150
Tr
M
C
B
155
– nit
– nit in no – mi – ne
– nit in no – mi – ne
160
Do – mi
Do – mi
165
Do – mi
170

175
Tr
ni;
C
ni;
B
ni;
180
Tr
O - - san
M
O - san -
C
O - san
B
O - san
185
Tr
na
M
C
B
na
190
Tr
in ex -
M
- na in ex -
C
- na in ex -
B
in ex

Tr
M
C
B
cel
cel
cel
cel
195
200
sis.
sis.
sis.
sis.

82 CHRISTOPHER TYE *Lord, let thy servant now depart in peace*

James Wrightson, ed., *The Wanley Manuscripts*, Recent Researches in the Music of the Renaissance, Part 1, vol. 99 (Madison, WI: A-R Editions, Inc., 1995), pp. 33–36.

19
For mine eyes have seen the Sav- i-our sent from thee.
For mine eyes have seen the Sav- i-our sent from thee.
Sav- i- our sent from thee.
sent from thee.
25
Whom thou hast pre- par- ed: be- fore the
Whom thou hast pre- par- ed: be- fore the
Whom thou hast pre- par- ed: be- fore the face of thy peo-
Whom thou hast pre- par- ed: be- fore the face, be- fore the face of thy
31
face of thy peo- ple. A light to light-
face of thy peo- ple. A light to light-
- ple, of thy peo- ple. A light to light-
peo- ple. A light to light-

36
- en the Gen-tiles: to be the glo- - ry of thy peo- ple of Is-
- en the Gen-tiles: to be the glo- ry of thy peo- - ple of Is-
- en the Gen-tiles: to be the glo- ry of thy peo- ple of Is- ra-
- en the Gen-tiles: to be the glo- - ry of thy peo- ple of Is- ra-
42
- ra- el. Glo- - ry to the
- ra- el. Glo- - ry to the Fa- ther, and
- el. Glo- ry to the Fa- ther, and
- el. Glo- ry to the Fa- - ther, and to the
48
Fa- ther, and to the Son: and to the Ho- ly Ghost;
to the Son: and to the Ho- ly Ghost;
to the Son: and to the Ho- ly Ghost, the Ho- ly Ghost;
Son, and to the Son: and to the Ho- ly Ghost;

54
As it was in the be- gin- ning, and is
As it was in the be- gin- ning, and is now, and ev- er shall
As it was in the be- gin- ning, and is now, and ev- er shall
As it was in the be- gin- - ning, and is now, and
60
now, and ev- er shall be: world with-out end, world with- out end.
[be:] world with- out end.
be: world with- out end.
ev- er shall be: world with- out end, world with- out end.
66
Al- way so be it, so be it.
Al- way so be it, so be it.
Al- way so be it, so be it.
Al- way so be it, so be it.

83 ORLANDE DE LASSUS *Prophetiae sibyllarum:* Prologue

Lassus, Orlando de. *Prophaetiae Sibyllarum.* Ed. Friedrich Blüme. In *Das Chorwerk* 48 (Wolfenbüttel: Georg Kallmeyer, 1937), p. 5. Used by permission of the publisher.

Carlo Gesualdo, *Sämtliche Madrigali*. Vol. 6. Ed. Weismann (Leipzig: VEB Deutscher Verlag für Musik, 1987), pp. 74–77. Used by permission of Breitkopf & Härtel, Wiesbaden.

13
- ta, e non vuol dar-mi a-i- - ta! Mo - ro, las - so, al
- ta, e non vuol dar-mi a-i- - ta! Mo - ro, las - so, al mio
i - ta, e non vuol dar - mi a - i - ta! Mo - ro, las - so, al mio
i - ta, e non vuol dar - mi a - i - ta! Mo - ro, las - so, al
i - ta, e non vuol dar - mi a - i - ta!
17
mio duo - lo E chi mi può dar vi- - - -
duo - - lo E chi mi può dar vi- - - - ta
duo - - lo E chi mi può dar vi- - - - - - ta, e chi mi
mio duo - lo E chi mi può dar vi- - - - ta, e
E chi mi può dar vi- - - ta, e chi
22
- ta, e chi mi può dar vi- - - - - ta, Ahi, che m'an-
e chi mi può dar vi- - - - - - ta, Ahi, che m'an-
può dar vi- - - - - - ta, Ahi, che m'anci- - -
chi mi può dar vi- - - - ta, Ahi, che m'an-
mi può dar vi- - - - - - ta, Ahi che m'an-ci- - -

26
ci - de e non vuol dar - mi a - i - ta, e non vuol dar - mi a - i - ta!
ci - de e non vuol dar - mi a-i - ta, e non vuol dar - mi a - i - ta! O
- de e non vuol dar - mi a - i - ta, e non vuol dar - mi a - i - ta! O
ci - de e non vuol dar-mi a-i - - ta, e non vuol darmi a i - - - ta!
de e non vuol dar - mi a - i - ta, e non vuol dar - mi a - i - ta! O do-lo-
30
O do - lo - ro - sa sor - te, Chi dar vi-
do - lo - ro - sa sor - te, o do - lo - ro - sa sor - te, Chi dar vi-
do - lo - ro - sa sor - te, o do - lo - ro - sa sor - te, Chi dar vi-
O do - lo - ro - sa sor - te, o do - lo - ro - - sa sor - - te, Chi dar vi-
ro - - sa sor - - te, Chi dar vi-
35
- ta mi può, ahi, mi dà mor - te, ahi,
- ta mi può, ahi, mi dà mor - te, ahi, mi dà mor - te,
- ta mi può, ahi, mi dà mor - te, ahi,
- ta mi può, ahi, mi dà mor te, ahi, mi dà mor-
- ta mi può, ahi, mi dà mor - -

39
— mi dà mor- - -te, ahi, ahi, mi dà mor - te!
ahi, mi dà mor - te, ahi,— mi dà mor- - - -te!
mi dà mor - te, ahi, mi dà mor - te, ahi, mi dà mor- - - -te!
- - te, ahi, mi dà mor - - te, ahi, mi dà mor - te!
te, ahi, mi dà mor- - - -te!

85a GIOVANNI PIERLUIGI DA PALESTRINA *Dum complerentur*

From Giovanni Pierluigi da Palestrina, *Le Opere Complete*, vol. 5, ed. Casimiri. Published by the Istituto Italiano per la Storia Della Musica, Rome. Used by permission.

20
- le-lú-ja,........... al - le - lú - ja, al - le-lú -
- le-lú-ja,........... al-le - lú - -ja, al-
al - le-lú - ja,..........
le - lú-ja, al - le- lú -ja,........ al - le-lú - ja,........... al - le-lú-
al - le-lú-ja,..................... al - le-lú - - ja,
al - le-lú-ja,..........
25
ja,............ al - le-lú - ja,.......... al - le - -
le - lú - ja, al - le-lú - - ja, al - le -
al - le-lú - ja,.......... al - le-lú - ja,........
ja,.......... al - le - lú - ja, al - le - lú-
al - le-lú-ja,........... al - le-lú -
al - le-lú - ja,........... al - le-lú - ja,........
30
35
lú - ja, et sú - bi-to, et sú - bi-to.......... fa -
lú - ja, et sú - bi-to, et sú - bi-to, et sú - bi-to
.... et sú - bi-to, et sú - bi-to
- - ja et sú - bi-to, et sú - bi - to, et sú - bi- to
- - ja, et sú - bi-to, et sú - bi-to, et sú - bi-to
al - le - lú - ja, et sú - bi-to, et sú - bi-to

40
-ctus est so- -nus de cœ- -lo, al-
fa-ctus est so- -nus, so- -nus de cœ - lo,
fa-ctus est so - -nus, so - nus de cœ lo, al-
fa-ctus est so - nus, so- -nus de cœ - lo, al-
fa-ctus est....... so- -nus, de.................. cœ - lo,
fa-ctus est so- -nus de cœ - lo,
45
le - lú - ja,.......... al - le - -lú - ja, al - le - lú - ja,.........
al - le - lú - -ja, al - le - lú - ja,....... al-
le - lú - ja,......... al- -le - lú - -ja, al - le - lú -
le - lú - ja,........ al - le - lú - ja, ... al-
al - le - lú - ja,.........
al - le - lú - ja,......... al - le - lú - ja,..........
50
.... al - le - lú - ja,.......... al - le - lú - ja,
le - lú - ja,......... al - le - lú - ja, al - le - lú - ja, tam-quam spí - ri-tus
ja,.................. al - le - - lú ja,
le - lú - ja,............ al - le - lú - ja, al - le - lú - ja, tam-quam spí - ri-tus
al - le - lú - ja,.......... al - le - lú - ja, tam-quam spí-ri - tus
al - le - lú - ja, al - le - lú - ja, tam-quam spí - ri-tus

tamquam spi - ri-tus ve-he- mén - tis, ve - he-mén - tis, et re-
ve - he-mén tis, et re-
tam - quam spí - ri-tus ve - he-mén - tis, et re-
ve - he-mén - tis, tamquam spi - ri-tus ve - he - mén - tis, ve - he-mén tis, et re-
vehemén - tis, spí - ri - tus ve - he - mén - - tis, et
ve - he-mén - tis, et re-
plé - vit to - tam do-mum, to - - tam do - mum, al-
plé - vit to - tam do - mum, do - mum, al-
plé - vit to - tam do - mum, to - tam do - mum
plé - vit to - tam do - mum, [do - mum,] al-
re - plé - vit to - tam do-mum, to - tam do - mum,
plé - vit to - tam do - mum, to - tam do - mum,
le - lú - ja,
le - lú ja, al -
al- le- lú-
le- lú - ja,
al - le - lú-
al - le -

75
al - le - lú - - ja,
- le - lú - ja, al- - le - - lú - - ja,
- - ja, al- - le - lú - ja, al- - le - lú-
al- - le - lú - - ja, al - le- - lú - ja,
- - ja, al- - le - lú-
- lú - ja, al- - le - lú - ja, al - - le -
80
al - le lú-ja, al - - le - lú - - ja.
al - le - lú - ja, al - le - lú - ja, al - - le lú - ja.
- - ja, al - le - lú - ja.
al- - le - lú - ja.
ja, al - - le - lú - - ja.
lú - ja, al - le - lú - ja, al - - le - lú - ja.
SECUNDA PARS.
CANTUS
ALTUS
SEXTUS (Altus II)
TENOR
QUINTUS (Tenor II)
BASSUS
5
Dum er - go es - sent
Dum er - go es - sent dum er - go es - sent
Dum er - go es - sent
Dum er - go es - sent dum er - go es -
Dum er - go es -
Dum er - go es -

10
in u- - num di - scí - pu - li con - gre - gá - -
in u- - num di - scí - pu - li con - gre - gá - -
in u- - num di - scí - pu - li con - gre - gá - -
sent in u- - num di - scí - pu - li con - gre-gá - - ti.....
sent in u- - num di - scí - pu - li con - gre - gá - -
sent in u- - num di - scí - pu - li con - gre - gá - -
15
ti pro - pter me - tum Iu - dæ - ó - rum,
ti pro - pter me - tum Iu - dæ - ó - rum, pro - pter me - tum
ti pro - pter me - tum Iu - dæ - ó - rum, pro - pter me - tum
.... pro - pter me - tum Iu - dæ - ó - rum,
ti pro - pter me - tum Iu-
ti pro - pter me - tum Iu-
20
so- nus re - pén- - te,
Iu - dæ - ó - rum so- nus re - pén- - te,
Iu - dæ - ó - rum so - nus re-pén -
so- nus re - pén - - te,.................
- dæ - ó - rum so - nus re - pén -
- dæ - ó - rum so - nus re-pén -

25
so - nus re-pen- - te de cœ- - lo
so - nus re-pen- - te de cœ - lo
- - te, so - nus re - pen - te de cœ- - lo
so - nus re- - pen - te de cœ - lo ve-
- te, de cœ - lo
- - te, de cœ - - lo
30
ve- - nit su - per e - os, ve -
ve- - nit su - per e - os, ve- -
ve - nit su - per e - os, ve -
- - nit su - per e - - os, su - per e - os, ve- -
ve - nit su - per e - os, ve - nit su - per e - os, ve-
ve - nit su - per e - os, ve -
35
- nit su - per e- - os
- nit su - per e - os tam-quam spí - ri-tus ve - he-men -
- nit su - per e- - os
nit su - per e- - os tam-quam spí - ri-tus ve - he - men -
- nit su - per e - os........ tam-quam spí - ri - tus vehemen- -
- nit su - per e- - os tam-quam spí - ri-tus ve - he - men -

40
tam-quam spí - ri-tus ve - he - men - tis, ve - he - men - tis, et re -
tis,
et re -
tam-quam spí - ri-tus ve - he - men - tis, et re -
tis, tam-quam spí - ri-tus ve - he - men - tis, ve - he - men - tis, et re -
tis, spí - ri - tus ve - he - men- - tis, et
tis,
et re -
45
plé - vit to - tam do-num, to- - tam do -
plé - vit to - tam do - num, do -
plé - vit to tam do - num, to - tam do -
plé - - vit to - tam do - num, do -
re - plé - vit to- - tam do-num, to - tam do-num. Al -
plé - vit to - tam do - num, to - - tam do -
50
num. Al - - le - - lú - - ja,
num. Al- le - - lú - ja,
num.
Al -
num.
Al -
- le - - lú ja,
num.
Al - - le -

55
al- -le - lú-
al- -le - lú - ja, al- -
- le- - lú- - ja, al- - le-
- - le- - lú- -ja,
al- - le - lú -
- - lú - ja, al- - le -
60
- - ja,
al - - le - lú-
le- - lú- - ja, al - le - lú - ja,
- lú - ja, al- - le - lú- - ja, [al-
al- - le - lú- - ja,
- - ja al - le- - lú - ja, al- - le-
lú- - ja, al - - le - lú- - ja, al - le -
65
ja, al- - le - lú- - ja.
[al - le - lú - ja,] al- - le - lú- - ja.
- le - lú - ja.]
al- - le - lú- - ja.
lú- - ja.
lú- - ja, al- - le - lú - ja.

85b GIOVANNI PIERLUIGI DA PALESTRINA *Missa Dum complerentur:* Gloria

 From Giovanni Pierluigi da Palestrina, *Le Opere Complete*, vol. 24, ed. Bianchi. Published by the Istituto Italiano per la Storia Della Musica, Rome. Used by permission.

20
-ti-as á- -gi-mus ti- - - - -bi
-ti-as á- -gi-mus ti- -bi pro-pterma-
-ti-as á- -gi-mus ti- -bi pro-pterma-
-ti-as á- -gi-mus ti- -bi
-ti-as á- - - - -mus ti- -bi pro-pterma-
-ti-as á- -gi-mus ti- -bi
25
pro-pterma-gnam gló-ri-am tu- - -
-gnam gló-ri-am tu- -am.
-gnam gló-ri-am tu-am, gló- - -ri-
pro-pterma-gnam gló-ri-am tu-am, gló-ri-am tu- - -
-gnam [pro-pterma-gnam] gló- - -
pro-pterma-gnam gló-
30
-am.
Dó-mi-ne De- - - - -us, Rex coe-lé-
-am tu-am. Dó-mi-ne De- -us, Rex coe-lé-
-am. Dó-mi-ne De-us, Rex coe-lé- - - - -
-ri-am tu-am.
-ri-am tu-am. Dó-mi-ne De-us, Rex coe-lé-

35
De - us Pa - ter o - mní - po - - - - - tens.
-stis, De - us Pa - ter o - mní - po - tens.
-stis, De - us Pa - ter Dó - mi-ne
-stis, De - us Pa - ter o - mní - po - tens. Dó - mi-ne
De - us Pa - ter o - mní - po - tens, o - mní - po - tens.
-stis, Dó - mi-ne
40
Je - - - su
Dó - mi-ne Fi - - li u - ni - gé - ni - te, Je - - - su
Fi - - - - - li u - ni - gé - ni - te, Je - su Chri-
Fi - - li Je - - - su
Dó - mi - ne Fi - li u - ni-gé-ni - te, Je - - - su
Fi - - li u - ni - gé - - ni - te, Je - - - - su
45
Chri - - ste. Dó - mi - ne De - us, A-gnus De - i, Dó - mi-ne De-us, A - gnus
Chri - - ste. Dó - mi-ne De-us, A-gnus De - i, Dó - mi - ne De-us, A - gnus
- - ste. Dó - mi-ne De - us, A-gnus De - i, A -
Chri - - ste. Dó - mi - ne De - us, A-gnus De - i,
Chri - - ste. Dó - mi - ne De-us, Dó - mi-ne De - us, A-gnus
Chri - - ste.

De - i, [Dó - mi-ne Dé - us, A-gnus De - i,] Fí - li-us Pa-
De - i, Fí - li-
-gnus De - i, Dó - mi-ne De-us, A-gnus De - i, Fí - li-us
Dó - mi-ne De- -us, A - gnus De - i,
De - i, Fí - li - us Pa-
Dó - mi-ne De - us, A-gnus De - i,
-tris, [Fí - li-us Pa- -tris.]
-us Pa- -tris, Fí- -li - us Pa- -tris.
Pa - tris, Fí- -li - us Pa- tris.
Fí - li - us Pa- -tris.
-tris, Fí - li - us Pa - tris.
Fí - li-us Pa- -tris.
Qui tol - lis pec-cá - ta mun - di, pec-cá - ta mun-di,
Qui tol-lis pec - cá- - ta mun-
Qui tol-lis pec - cá- -ta mun-
Qui tol - lis pec- cá - ta mun-

65
mi - - - se - ré - re no - - - bis.
mi - - - se - ré - re no - - - bis.
di, mi - - se - ré - re no - - - - bis. Qui
di, mi - - se - ré - - re no - bis.
di, mi - - se - ré - re no - - - bis. Qui
mi - - - se - ré - re no - - - bis.
70
Qui tol - lis pec - cá - ta mun - di,
Qui tol - lis pec - cá - ta mun - di, pec - cá - -
tol - - lis pec - cá - ta mun - - - - di,
Qui tol - lis pec - cá - ta mun - di, [qui tol -
tol - lis pec - cá - ta mun - di, [qui tol -
Qui tol - lis pec -
75
sú - sci - pe de - pre - ca - ti -
ta mun - di, sú - sci - pe de - pre - ca - ti -
sú - sci - pe de - pre - ca - ti -
lis pec - cá - ta mun - di,] sú - sci - pe de - pre - ca - ti - ó -
lis pec - cá - ta mun - di,] sú - sci - pe de - pre - ca - ti -
cá - ta mun - di, sú - sci - pe

80
-ó- - - - - - -nem no - stram. Qui se - des
-ó- - - - - - -nem no- - - - - -stram.Qui se - des
-ó- - - - - - -nem no- - - -stram.Qui se - des ad
- - - - - -nem no- - - -stram. Qui se - des ad
-ó- - - - - -nem no- - - - - -stram. Qui se - des
de - pre - ca-ti-ó - nem no - stram.Qui se - des ad
85
ad déx-te - ram Pa- - - - -
ad déx-te - ram Pa- -
déx-te-ram Pa - tris, ad déx-te - ram Pa- - - - -
déx-te-ram Pa - tris,
ad déx - te - ram, [ad déx - te - ram] Pa - tris, ad déx - te - ram Pa-tris,
déx-te - ram Pa - tris,
90
-tris, mi - se - ré-re no - - - - - -
-tris, mi - se - ré-re no- - -bis, mi- - -se - ré- - -re
-tris, mi- - -se - ré - re no- - -bis, mi - se-
mi - se-ré - re no- -bis, mi- - -se - ré-re
mi- -se - ré-re no- -bis, mi - se-ré- -re no- -
mi - se - ré - re, [mi - se-ré - re,] mi - se-ré-re

95
- - - - bis. Quó - ni - am tu so - lus san - - -
no - - - bis. Quó - ni - am
- ré - re no - bis. Quó - ni - am tu so - lus san - - - -
no - - bis Quó - ni - am
- bis. Quó - ni - am tu so - lus san - - - -
no - - - - bis. Quó - ni - am
100
- - ctus. Tu so - lus Dó - - - - mi -
tu so - lus Dó - - - - - mi - nus.
- - ctus. Tu so - lus Dó - mi - nus.
tu so - lus san - - - - - ctus. Tu so - lus
- - ctus. Tu so - lus Dó - mi - nus,
tu so - lus Dó - - - - mi - nus.
105
- nus, Dó - - - - mi - nus. Tu so - lus, [tu
Tu so - - lus Al - - tís - - si - mus,
Tu so - lus Al - tís - si - mus, tu
Dó - - - - - mi - nus. Tu so - lus, [tu so -
Dó - - - - mi - nus. Tu so - lus Al - tís - si - mus,
Tu so - lus Al - tís - si - mus,

110
so - lus] Al - tís - si - mus, Je - su Chri -
Je - - su Chri -
so - lus Al - tís - si - mus, Je - su Chri -
- lus] Al - tís - si - mus, Je - su Chri - ste, Je - su
Je - su Chri -
Je - su Chri -
115
- ste. Cum San - cto Spí - ri - tu
- ste. Cum San - cto Spí - ri - tu, cum
- ste Cum San -
Chri - ste. Cum San - cto Spí - ri - tu, cum
- ste. Cum San - cto Spí - ri - tu
- ste. Cum San -
120
in gló - ri - a De -
San - cto Spí - ri - tu
- cto Spí - ri - tu in gló - ri - a De - i Pa -
San - cto Spí - ri - tu
in gló - ri - a De - i
- cto Spí - ri - tu

125
-i Pa - tris. A - men, in gló - ri -
in gló - ri - a De - i Pa-
-tris. A- - - - -men,
in gló- -ri - a De - i
Pa - tris. A- - -men, a- - -men,
in gló- - -ri - a De -
130
-a De - i Pa- - - tris. A - men, in gló- -
-tris. A- - -men, in gló- - - -ri - a
in gló- - ri - a De - i
Pa - tris. A- - -men, in gló- - -ri - a
in gló - ri - a De - i
-i. Pa- - -tris. A - men, in gló- - -ri -
135
- -ri - a De- - -i Pa - tris. A - men.
De- -i Pa - tris. A - men.
Pa - tris. A - men, a- - -men.
De - i Pa - tris. A - men.
Pa - tris. A - men, De - i Pa - tris. A - men.
-a De - i Pa- - -tris. A- - -men.

86 GIOVANNI PIERLUIGI DA PALESTRINA *Nigra sum*

almost chordal

20
rú-sa-lem,] sic - ut ta-ber-ná-cu-
lem,] sic - ut ta-ber-ná-cu-la Ce-dar,
sic - ut ta-ber-ná-cu-la Ce-dar, sic - ut ta-ber-ná-cu-la Ce-
Je-rú-sa-lem, sic - ut ta-ber-ná-cu-la Ce-dar, sic-ut ta-
sic - ut ta-ber-ná-cu-la Ce-dar, sic-
25
la Ce-dar, sic - ut pel - les
sic-ut ta - ber-ná-cu - la Ce-dar, sic - ut pel-les
dar, Ce-dar, sic - ut pel - les Sa-lo-mó - nis,
ber-ná-cu-la Ce-dar, sic - ut pel - les Sa-lo-mó - nis,
- ut ta-ber-ná-cu-la Ce - dar, sic. - ut pel - les
80
85
Sa-lo-mó - nis, Sa-lo-mó - nis.
Sa - lo-mó - nis, sic - ut pel - les Sa-lo-mó -
[sic - ut pel - les Sa-lo-mó - nis,] Sa - lo-mó -
sic - ut pel - les Sa-lo-mó -
[sic - ut pel - les] Sa-lo-mó -

40
No - lí - te me con-si-de - rá - re quod fu-sca sim, quod fu-sca
- nis. No - lí - te me con-si-de - rá - re quod fu-sca sim,
- nis. No - lí - te me con-si-de - rá - re quod fu-sca sim, quod fu-sca
nis. No - lí - te me con-si-de - rá - re quod fu-sca sim, quod fu-sca
nis. No - lí - te me con-si-de - rá - re quod fu-sca
45
sim, qui - a de - co - lo - rá - vit me sol: fí - li - i
qui - a de - co - lo - rá - vit me sol: fi - lí - i ma -
sim, qui - a de - co - lo - rá - vit me sol: fí - li - i ma -
sim, qui - a de - co - lo - rá - vit me sol: fí - li - i
sim, qui - a fí - li - i
50
ma - tris me - æ pu - gna - vé - runt contra me, pu -
- tris me - æ pu - gna - vé - runt contra me, pu -
- tris me - æ pu - gna - vé - runt contra me,
ma - tris me - æ pu - gna - vé - runt contra me, pu -
ma - tris me - æ pu - gna - vé - runt contra me,

55
- gna - vé - runt contra me, po - su - é - runt me,
- gna - vé - runt contra me, po - su - é - runt me cu - stó - dem in ví -
po - su - é - runt me cu - stó - dem in
- gna - vé - runt contra me, po - su - é - runt me cu - stó - dem in
po - su - é - runt me cu - stó - dem in
60
po - su - é - runt me cu - stó - dem in ví - ne - is,
- ne - is, po - su - é - runt me cu - stó - dem in ví - ne - is,
ví - ne - is, po - su - é - runt me cu - stó - dem in ví - ne - is, po -
ví - ne - is, po - su - é - runt me cu - stó - dem in ví - ne -
ví - ne - is, po - su - é - runt me,
65
po - su - é - runt me cu - stó - dem in ví - ne - is.
po - su - é - runt me cu - stó - dem in ví - ne - is.
- su - é - runt me cu - stó - dem in ví - ne - is.
is, po - su - é - runt me cu - stó - dem in ví - ne - is.
po - su - é - runt me cu - stó - dem in ví - ne - is.

87a TOMÁS LUIS DE VICTORIA Requiem Mass: Agnus Dei

18
A-gnus De - i,
qui tol - - - - - - lis, qui tol - lis
qui tol - - - lis pec - - - - - ca -
qui tol - - - lis, qui tol - - - - lis pec - ca - ta
qui tol - - - lis pec -
qui tol - - - lis pec - ca - ta
qui tol - - - lis pec -
23
pec - ca - ta mun - - - di, do - na e -
-ta mun - - - di, do - - - na e - - - is
mun - - - - - - - - - di, do - na e - is re - qui - em, do -
-ca - ta mun - - - - - - di, do - na e - is re - qui -
mun - - - - - - - - - - di, do - na e - is re - qui -
-ca - ta mun - - - - - - - di, do - - - - na e - is re - qui -
30
-is re - qui - em sem - - - pi - - - ter - nam, sem - pi - ter - - - nam.
re - qui - em sem - - - pi - ter - nam, sem - pi - ter - nam.
- na e - is re - qui - em sem - pi - ter - - - - nam, sem - pi - ter - nam.
-em sem - pi - ter - nam, sem - - - - - - - pi - ter - nam.
-em sem - pi - ter - nam, sem - pi - ter - nam, sem - pi - ter - - - - nam.
-em sem - pi - ter - nam, sem - pi - ter - nam, sem - pi - ter - nam.

87b TOMÁS LUIS DE VICTORIA Requiem Mass: *Versa est in luctum*

19
-ra me - a, et or - ga - num me - - - - - - - - - - um:
me - - - - a, et or - ga - num me - - - - - - um:
- tha-ra me - - - a, in vo-cem
- tha-ra me - a, et or - ga - num me - - - - - - um: in vo-cem
ci - tha-ra me - a, in vo-cem
-tha - ra me - a, in vo-cem
25
Par - - - - ce mi - hi, Do - - - - mi - ne,
in vo-cem flen - - - - - ti - um: par - - - - ce
flen - ti - um: Par - - - ce mi - hi, Do - - -
flen - ti - um, in vo-cem flen - - - - ti - um: par -
flen - ti - um, Par - ce mi - hi,
flen - ti - um: par - - - - - ce mi - hi Do - - - - mi - ne,
31
par - ce mi - hi, Do - - - - mi - ne, ni - hil e - nim sunt di - es
mi - hi, Do - - - - - mi - ne, ni - hil e - nim
- mi - ne, par - ce mi - - - hi, Do - mi - ne,
- - - ce mi - hi, Do - - - - mi - ne ni - - - hil e - nim
par - - - ce mi - - hi, Do - mi - ne, ni - hil e - nim
par - - - ce mi - hi, Do - mi - ne,

37
me - i, ni - hil e - nim sunt di - es me - i, di - es me - i,
sunt di - es me - i, ni - hil e - nim sunt di -
ni - hil e - nim sunt di - es me - i, ni - hil
sunt di - - es me - - - - i, ni - hil e - nim sunt di - es
sunt di - es me - i, ni - hil e - nim sunt di - es me - - -
ni - - hil e - nim sunt di - - es me - - - - i, di -
43
ni - hil e - nim sunt di - - es me - - - - i,
- es me - - - - - - i, ni - hil e - nim sunt di - - - es me -
e - nim sunt di - - - - - es me - - - - i, di - es me - - - - i, ni -
me - i, di - es me - i, di - es me - - - - i, ni -
- i, di - es me - - - - i, ni - hil e - nim sunt
es me - - - - - - i, ni - - - hil e - nim sunt di - - - - es me -
49
ni - hil e - nim sunt di - es me - - - - - - i, ni - hil e - nim sunt
- i, ni - hil e - nim sunt
- hil e - nim sunt di - es me - - - - - - - - i, ni - hil e - nim sunt
- hil e - nim sunt di - es me - - - - i, ni - hil e - nim sunt di -
ni - hil e - nim sunt
- i, ni - hil e - nim sunt

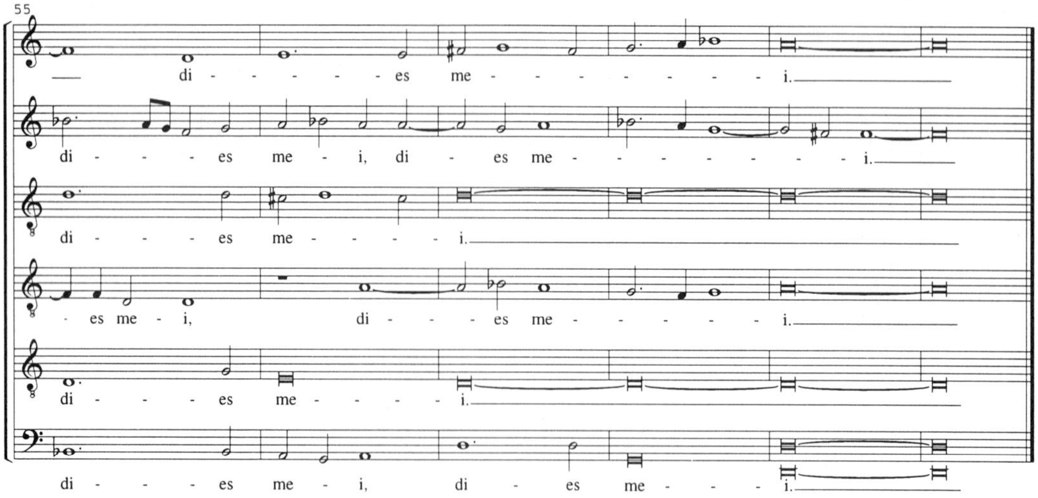
55
di - - - - - - es me - - - - - - - - i.
di - - - es me - i, di - es me - - - - - - - - i.
di - - - es me - - - - i.
- es me - i, di - - - es me - - - - - - - i.
di - - - - es me - - - - - i.
di - - - - es me - i, di - es me - - - i.

88 CLAUDE LE JEUNE *La bel' aronde*

La bel'aronde *(etc.)*

2. Quand nou quitant tu depars,
Aronde, mais ou vas-tu?
La ou revient le dous tans
D'ou les orages s'en vont.

La bel'aronde *(etc.)*

3. Lors que tu voles amont,
Alés vela le beau tans,
Et quand tu voles en bas,
Il plouvera, cachés vous.

La bel'aronde *(etc.)*

4. Ingenieuze tu sais
Plaquér ton aire, par fois
Sou les solives, par fois
Aus cheminé' l'agensant.

La bel'aronde *(etc.)*

5. L'air de la peste ne nuit
La ou tu fais ta maison.
Aporte nous la santé,
Vien, niche dans ma maison.

La bel'aronde *(etc.)*

89 ORLANDE DE LASSUS *Cum essem parvulus*

20
fa - ctus sum
fa - ctus sum
- - do au - tem fa - - ctus sum
- - do au - tem fa - ctus sum vir,
- - do au - tem fa - ctus sum
- do au - - - tem fa - ctus sum vir,
25
vir, e - va - cu - a - vi quae e - rant par - -
vir, e - va - cu - a - vi quae e - rant par -
vir, e - va - cu - a - vi quae e - rant:
e - va - cu - a - vi quae e - - rant:
vir, e - va - cu - a - vi quae e - rant:
e - va - cu - a - vi quae e - rant:
30
- - vu - li:
- - vu - li: vi - de - mus nunc per spe - cu -
vi - de - mus nunc per spe - - - -
vi - de - mus nunc per spe -
vi - de - mus nunc per spe - cu - lum

35
in ae-ni - gma-te, tunc au - tem, tunc
lum in ae-ni - gma-te, tunc au - tem, tunc au -
in ae-ni - gma-te, tunc au - tem, tunc au -
- cu-lum, tunc au - tem, tunc au - tem, tunc
- cu-lum, tunc au - tem, tunc au - tem
in ae-ni - gma-te, tunc au - tem, tunc
40
au - tem fa - ci-e ad fa - ci-em, fa - ci - e ad fa - ci - em.
tem, tunc au - tem fa - ci-e ad fa - ci-em, fa - ci - e ad fa - ci - em.
tem fa - ci-e ad fa - ci-em, fa - ci - e ad fa - ci - em.
au - tem fa - ci-e ad fa - ci-em, fa - ci - e ad fa - ci - em.
fa - ci-e ad fa - ci-em, fa - ci - e ad fa - ci - em.
au - tem fa - ci-e ad fa - ci-em, fa - ci - e ad fa - ci - em.
Secunda pars
45
Nunc co-gno - sco ex par - - - te,
Nunc co-gno - sco ex par - - - te,
Nunc co-gno - sco ex par - - - te,
Nunc
Nunc
Nunc

50
tunc au - tem co-
tunc au - - tem co-
tunc au - tem co -
co-gno - sco ex par - - - - te, tunc au - tem co-
co-gno - sco ex par - - - - te, tunc au - tem co-
co-gno - sco ex par - - - - te, tunc au - tem co -
55
gno-scam sic - ut, sic - ut et co - gni - tus
gno-scam sic - ut et co - gni-tus sum.
gno-scam sic - ut, sic - ut et co - gni-
gno - scam sic - ut et co-gni - tus sum, et co - gni-
gno-scam sic - ut et co - gni-tus sum.
gno - scam sic - ut et co - gni-
60
sum. Fi - - - - - - -
Nunc au - tem ma - nent Fi -
tus sum. Nunc au - tem ma-nent Fi - des,
tus sum. Nunc au-tem ma-nent Fi - - - -
Nunc au - tem ma-nent Fi - - -
tus sum. Fi - des,

65
des, Spes, Cha - ri - tas, tri - -
- des, Spes, Cha - ri - tas:
Fi - des, Spes, Cha - ri - tas, tri -
des, Spes, Cha - ri - tas, tri -
des, Spes, Cha - ri - tas:
Spes, Cha - ri - tas:
70
a haec: ma - - jor au-tem, ma -
ma - jor au - tem, ma-jor au - tem,
- a haec: ma - - jor au - -
- a haec: ma - - jor au - tem,
ma - jor au - tem, ma -
ma - - jor au -
75
- - - jor au - tem ho - rum est Cha - ri -
ma - - jor au-tem ho - rum est
- tem, ma - jor au - tem ho - rum est Cha -
ma - - jor au - tem ho - rum est Cha -
- - jor au - tem ho - rum est Cha -
- tem, ma - jor au - tem ho - rum est

80
tas, Cha - ri - tas, Cha - ri - tas.
— Cha - ri - tas, Cha - ri - tas, Cha - ri - tas.
- ri - tas, Cha - ri - tas, Cha - ri - tas.
- ri - tas, Cha - ri - tas, Cha - ri - tas.
- ri - tas, Cha - ri - tas, Cha - ri - tas.
Cha - ri - tas, Cha - ri - tas.

90 ORLANDE DE LASSUS *La nuict froide et sombre*

19
vant, Au la - beur dui - sant, au la - beur dui - sant Sa lu - eur ex -
sui - vant, Au la - beur dui - sant, au la - beur dui - sant Sa lu - eur ex -
Puis le jour sui - vant, Au la - beur dui - sant Sa lu - eur ex -
sui - vant, puis la jour sui - vant, Au la - beur dui - sant Sa lu - eur ex -
22
po - se; Et d'un tein di - vers, et d'un tein di - vers,
po - se; Et d'un tein di - vers, et d'un tein di - vers, Ce
po - se; Et d'un tein di - vers,
po - se; Et d'un tein di - vers,
25
Ce grand u - ni - vers. Ta - pis - se et com - po - se,
grand u - ni - vers. Ta - pis - se et com - po - se, ta -
Ce grand u - ni - vers. Ta - pis - se et com - po - se,
Ce grand u - ni - vers. Ta - pis - se et com - po - se, ta -
28
ta - pis - se et com - po - se, ta - pis - se et com - po - se, ta - pis -
pis - se et com - po - se, ta - pis - se et com - po - se, ta - pis - se et com - po -
ta - pis - se et com - po - se, ta - pis - se et com - po - se,
pis - se et com - po - se, ta - pis - se et com - po - se, ta -
31
se et com - po - se, ta - pis - se et com - po - se.
se, ta - pis - se et com - po - se, ta - pis - se et com - po - se.
ta - pis - se et com - po - se, ta - pis - se et com - po - se.
pis - se et com - po - se, ta - pis - se et com - po - se.

91 CIPRIANO DE RORE *Da le belle contrade d'oriente*

20
pia - cer che non ca - pe hu - ma - - na men - te,
cer che non ca - - pe hu - ma - na men - - te, Quan - do sen -
pia - cer che non ca - pe hu - ma - na men - - - - - te, Quan - do sen -
cer che non ca - - pe hu - ma - - na men - - - te, Quan - do sen -
cer che non ca - pe hu - ma - - na men - te, Quan - do sen -
25
Spe - ran - za del mio cor, dol - ce
tii do - po un so - spir ar - den - te: Spe - ran - za del mio cor, dol -
tii do - po un so - spir ar - den - te: Spe - ran - za del mio cor, dol -
tii do - po un so - spir ar - den - te: Spe - ran - za del mio cor,
tii do - po un so - spir ar - den - te: Spe - ran - - za del mio cor, dol -
30
de - si - - o, Te'n vai, hai - me, so - la mi la - sci, a -
- ce de - si - o, Te'n vai, hai - me, te'n vai, hai - me, a - di - o.
ce de - si - o, Te'n vai, hai - me, a - di - o.
Te'n vai, hai - me, a -
ce de - si - o, Te'n vai, hai - me, hai - me, a - di - o.
35
40
di - o. Che sa - rà qui di me scu - ra e do - len - - te?
Che sa - rà qui di me scu - ra e do - len - te?
Che sa - rà qui di me scu - ra e do - len - te?
di - o. Che sa - rà qui di me scu - ra e do - len - te?

45
Ahi cru - do A - mor, ahi cru - do A - mor, ben son du - bio - se e
Ahi cru - do A - mor, ahi cru - do A - mor, ben son du - bio - se e
Ahi cru - do A - mor, ahi cru - do A - mor, ben son du - bio - se e
Ahi cru - do A - mor,
Ahi cru - do A - mor, ben son du - bio - se e
50
cor - te Le tue dol - cez - ze, poi - ch'an - cor ti go - di Che l'e - stre -
cor - te Le tue dol - cez - ze, poi - ch'an - cor ti go - di Che l'e - stre - - -
cor - te Le tue dol - cez - ze, poi - ch'an - cor ti go - di Che l'e - stre - mo pia -
Che l'e - stre - mo pia -
cor - te Le tue dol - cez - ze, poi - ch'an - cor ti go - di Che l'e - stre - mo pia -
55
mo pia - cer fi - ni - - sca in pian - to. Nè po - ten -
mo pia - cer fi - ni - sca in pian - to. Nè po - ten - do dir più, nè po - ten -
cer fi - ni - sca in pian - - to. Nè po -
cer fi - ni - sca in pian - to. Nè po - ten - do dir più,
cer fi - ni - sca in pian - - to. Nè po - ten - do dir più, nè po - ten -
60
do dir più, cin - se - me for - te, cin - se - me for - te, I - te - ran - do gl'am - ples - si,
do dir più, cin - se - me for - te, cin - se - me for - te, I - te - ran - do gl'am -
ten - do dir più, cin - se - me for - te, cin - se - me for - te, I - te -
cin - se - me for - te, cin - se - me for - te, I - te - ran - do gl'am - ples - si in tanti no -
do dir più, cin - se - me for - te, cin - se - me for - te, I - te - ran - do gl'am - ples - si,

65
i - te - ran - do gl'am - ples - si in tan - ti no - - - - - - di, Che gia - mai ne fer
ples - si, i - te - ran - do gl'am - ples - si in tan - ti no - di, Che gia- mai ne fer
ran - do gl'am - ples - - si in tan - ti no - di, in tan - ti no - di, Che
di, in tan - ti no - di, I - te - ran - do gl'am - ples - si in tan - ti no - di, Che gia-mai ne fer
i - te - ran - do gl'am - ples - si in tan - ti no - di,
70
più, che gia-mai ne fer più l'e - dra o l'a - can - - - - - - to,
più, che gia - mai ne fer più l'e - dra o l'a - can - to, l'e - dra o l'a -
gia - mai ne fer più l'e - dra o l'a - can - - - -
più, che gia - mai ne fer più l'e - dra o l'a - can - to,
Che gia - mai ne fer più l'e - dra o l'a - can - to, l'e - dra o l'a -
75
80
Che gia-mai ne fer più l'e - dra o l'a - can - - - - - to.
can - to, Che gia - mai ne fer più l'e - dra o l'a - can - to, l'e - dra o l'a - can - to.
- - to, Che gia - mai ne fer più l'e - dra o l'a - can - to.
Che gia - mai ne fer più l'e - dra o l'a - can - to.
can - to, Che gia - mai ne fer più l'e - dra o l'a - can - to.

92 LUCA MARENZIO *Scaldava il sol*

Cannon, Johnson, and Waite, *The Art of Music* (New York: Harper & Row, 1960), pp. 189–93.

15
on, Nel dor- so del Le- on suoalber- go ca- ro
dor- so del Le- on suoal- ber- go ca- ro
on suoalber- go ca- ro, suoal- ber- go ca- ro
on suoalber- go ca- ro
suoalber- go ca- ro
Sot- to'l bo- schet- to più di frondi car- co,
Sot- to'l bo- schet- to più di frondi
più di frondi car- co,
Sot- to'l bo- schet- - to
Sot- to'l bo- schet- - to più di
20
più di frondi car- - co.
car- co, più di frondi car- - co Dor-
più di frondi car- - - - co Dor-
più di frondi car- - co Dor- mia'l
fron- - di car- - co Dor-

25
mia'l pa- stor con le sue greggi a pa- ro Gia-
mia'l pa- stor con le sue greggi a pa- ro Gia-
mia'l pa- stor con le sue greggi a pa- ro Gia-
pa- stor Gia-
mia'l pa- stor con le sue greggia pa- ro Gia-
30
ce- va il villa-nel, il vil-la-
ce- va il villa-nel, il vil-la-
ce- vail vil-la-nel, il vil-la-nel
ce- vail vil-la-nel, il vil-la-nel
ce- va, Gia- ce- va
35
nel de l'o- pra scar- co Vie più di po-
nel de l'o- pra scar- co Vie più di po-
de l'o- pra scar- co Vie più di po-
de l'o- pra scar- co Vie più di po-

sa Gl'au-
sa che di spi- - - ghe a- va- ro Gl'au-
sa che di spighe a- va- - - ro Gl'au-
sa che di spi- - - ghe a-va- ro Gl'au-
- che di spi- - - ghe a-va- ro
gei, Gl'au-gei le fe- re ogn'huom s'a-
gei, Gl'au-gei le fe- - re o-
gei, Gl'au-gei le fe- re
gei, Gl'au-gei le fe- -
Gl'au-gei le fe- - re
scon- - de, ogn'huom s'a- scon- - - de
gn'huom, o- gn'huom s'a- scon-de e ta- ce,
ogn'huom s'a- scon- - - - - de e
re o- gn'huom ogn'huom s'a- scon- de e
ogn'huom s'a- scon- - - de e

55
e ta- ce Sol la Ci- ca-
e ta- ce Sol, Sol la Ci- ca-
ta- ce, e ta- ce Sol la Ci- ca-
ta- ce Sol
ta- ce Sol
60
la non si sen-tein pa- ce, non si sen-tein
la non si sen-tein pa- ce,
la non si sen-tein pa- ce, non si sen-tein
non si sen-tein pa- ce, non si sen-tein
non si sen-tein pa- ce,
65
pa- ce, non si sen-tein pa- ce.
non si sen-tein pa- ce.
pa- ce, non si sen-tein pa- ce.
pa- ce, non si sen-tein pa- ce.
non si sen-tein pa- ce.

93 ORAZIO VECCHI *Caro dolce mio bene*

2. Alma cara e gradita,
Refuggio di mia vita,
Quelle labbia rosate
Fate ch'io baci in foggie disusate.

3. Voi, caro il mio contento,
Rimedio al mio tormento,
Quei pomi acerbi ancora
Fate ch'io gusti prima ch'io mi mora.

4. E quel d'avorio petto
Fate ch'io tenga stretto
Sin ch'i messi d'Amore
Ambo sentiamo in amoroso ardore.

Ruth I. DeFord, ed., *Orazio Vecchi: The Four-Voice Canzonettas with Original Texts and Contrafacta by Valentin Haussmann and Others*, part 2, Recent Researches in the Music of the Renaissance, vol. 93 (Madison, WI: A-R Editions, Inc., 1993), PP. 92–93, 136–37.

94 MADDALENA CASULANA *Ahi possanza d'amor*

15
for-te gri-do ai-ta al mio pe-rir; poi mor-te
for-te gri-do ai-ta al mio pe-rir; poi mor-te
for-te gri-do ai-ta al mio pe-rir; poi mor-te
for-te gri-do ai-ta al mio pe-rir; poi mor-te
chie-gio. Co-sì ser-vo d'al-trui fe-li-ce a-spet-
chie-gio. Co-sì ser-vo d'al-trui fe-li-ce a-spet-
chie-gio. Co-sì ser-vo d'al-trui fe-li-ce, fe-
chie-gio. Co-sì ser-vo d'al-trui
20
to. Co-sì ser-vo d'al-trui fe-
to, fe-li-ce a-spet-to. Co-sì ser-vo d'al-trui fe-
li-ce a-spet-to. Co-sì ser-vo d'al-trui fe-
fe-li-ce a-spet-to. Co-sì ser-vo d'al-trui
li-ce a-spet-to.
li-ce a-spet-to, fe-li-ce a-spet-to.
li-ce, fe-li-ce a-spet-to.
fe-li-ce a-spet-to.

95 THOMAS TALLIS *In ieiunio et fletu*

par - ce po - pu-lo tu - o, par-ce po - pu-lo
- ne, par-ce po - pu-lo tu- - o, par-ce po - pu-lo tu- - - -
- ne, Do-mi - ne, par-ce po - pu-lo tu- - -
- ne, par-ce po - pu-lo tu - o, par-ce po - pu-lo tu - - o,
- ne, par-ce po - pu-lo tu - o, par-ce po - pu-lo tu- - -
tu - o, et ne des he - re-di-ta-tem tu-am in per-di - ti - o - nem,
- - o, et ne des he - re-di-ta-tem tu-am in per-di-ti-o - nem, he-re-di -
- o, et ne des he-re - di - ta - tem tu - am in per-di - ti-o-nem, he-re-di -
et ne des he-re-di - ta-tem tu-am in per-di-ti - o - nem, he-re-di -
- o, et ne des he-re-di -
he - re - di - ta - tem tu - am in per-di - ti -
- ta-tem tu-am in per-di - ti - o - nem, he - re - di - ta-tem tu - am in
- ta - tem tu-am in per-di - ti-o - nem, he - re - di - ta - tem tu - am in
- ta-tem tu-am in per-di - ti - o - nem, he - re - di-ta-tem tu-am in per -
- ta-tem tu-am in per-di - ti - o - nem, he - re-di-ta-tem tu-am in per-di -

- o - - nem: in- -ter ve-sti - bu-lum et al - ta - re plo-
per - di-ti-o - nem: in - ter ve-sti - bu-lum et al - ta - re
per - di-ti-o - nem: in - ter ve-sti - bu-lum et al - ta - re
-di - ti - o - nem: in - ter ve-sti - bu-lum et al - ta - re
-ti - o - - nem: in - ter ve-sti - bu-lum et al - ta - re
-ra - bant sa - cer-do - tes, di-cen - tes, Par - ce po-pu-lo tu-
plo-ra-bant sa-cer-do - tes, di - cen - - tes, Par - ce populo
plo-ra - bant sa - cer - do - tes, di - cen - - tes, Par - ce po - pu-
plo-ra - bant sa - cer - do - tes, di - cen - tes,
plo-ra - bant sa - cer - do - tes, di - cen - tes,
- - - o, par- -ce po - pu-lo tu - - o,
tu- - - - - o po - pu-lo tu - - o, par-
- lo tu - - - o, par - ce po - pu -
Par - ce po-pu - lo tu- - - - o, par - ce
Par - ce po-pu - lo tu- - o, par ce

par - ce po-pu-lo tu - - - - - - - - -
- ce po-pu-lo tu-o, par-ce po-pu-lo tu- - o, par-
- lo tu- - o, par - ce po - pu-lo tu- - - - -
po-pu-lo tu- - o, par - ce po-pu - lo tu- - - -
po-pu-lo tu - o, par - ce po-pu-
- o, par - ce po-pu-lo tu- - - - -
- ce po-pu-lo tu- - - - - - o, po-pu-lo tu- -
- - o, par - ce po - pu-lo, par-ce po - pu-lo tu - o, par-
- o, par - ce po-pu-lo tu- - - o, par - ce po-pu-lo tu-
- lo tu- - - - o,
- o, par - ce po-pu - lo tu- - - - o.
- o, par - ce po-pu-lo tu- - - - - o.
- - ce po-pu-lo tu- - - o, par - ce po-pu - lo tu- - - o.
- - - - - - o, par- ce po-pu-lo tu - o.
par - ce po-pu-lo tu - o, par - ce po-pu-lo tu- - - o.

96 WILLIAM MUNDY *O Lord, the maker of all things*

Peter Le Huray, ed., *The Treasury of English Church Music, 1545–1650* (Cambridge: Cambridge University Press, 1982), pp. 22–27.

10
Us to de - fend through thy mer - cy
Us to de - fend through thy mer - cy From
mer - cy, thy mer - cy From all de - ceits of our
- fend through thy mer - cy, through thy mer - cy From all de -

15
p DEC.
From all de - ceits of our e - ne - mies, of our e - ne - mies; Let
all de - ceits of our e - ne - mies, of our e - ne - mies; Let
e - ne - mies, from all de - ceits of our e - ne - mies; Let
- ceits of our e - ne - mies, of our e - ne - mies; Let

CAN.
20
DEC.
nei - ther us de - lud - ed be, Good Lord, with dream or fan - ta - sy, Our
nei - ther us de - lud - ed be, Good Lord, with dream or fan - ta - sy, Our
nei - ther us de - lud - ed be, Good Lord, with dream or fan - ta - sy, Our
nei - ther us de - lud - ed be, Good Lord, with dream or fan - ta - sy, Our

CAN.
hearts wak - ing in thee thou keep, That we in sin fall not on sleep,—
hearts wak - ing in thee thou keep, That we in sin fall not on sleep,—
hearts wak - ing in thee thou keep, That we in sin fall not on sleep,—
hearts wak - ing in thee thou keep, That we in sin fall not on sleep,—

25
FULL p
1st mf 2nd f
that we in sin fall not on sleep. O Fa - ther, through thy
FULL p
1st mf 2nd f
that we in sin fall not on sleep. O Fa - ther,
FULL p
1st mf 2nd f
that we in sin fall not on sleep. O
FULL p
that we in sin fall not on sleep.
1st mf 2nd f
p

30
bless - ed Son Grant us this our pe - ti - ti - on,
through thy bless - ed Son Grant us this our pe - ti - ti - on,
Fa - ther, through thy bless - ed Son Grant us this our pe - ti - ti - on,
1st mf 2nd f
O Fa - ther, through thy bless - ed Son Grant us this our pe -

35
grant us this___ our pe - ti - ti - on, To whom with the Ho -
grant us this___ our pe - ti - ti - on, To whom with the Ho -
grant us this___ our pe - ti - ti - on, To whom with the Ho - ly
- ti - ti - on our___ pe - ti - ti - on, To whom with the Ho -
(♭)

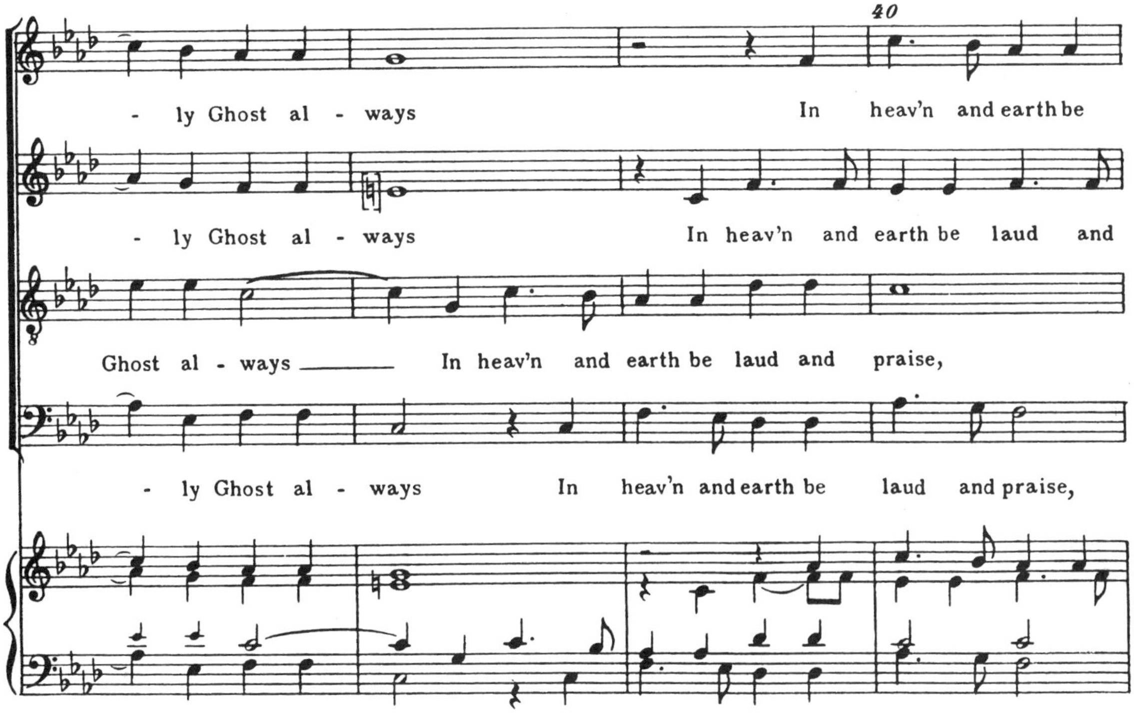
40
- ly Ghost al - ways In heav'n and earth be
- ly Ghost al - ways In heav'n and earth be laud and
Ghost al - ways ______ In heav'n and earth be laud and praise,
- ly Ghost al - ways In heav'n and earth be laud and praise,
(♮)

1
45
D.al.𝄋
laud and praise, in heav'n and earth be laud and praise. O
A1
praise, be laud and praise, in heav'n and earth be laud and praise.
A2
praise, be laud and praise, in heav'n and earth be laud and praise.
in heav'n and earth be laud and praise, be laud and praise.
in heav'n and earth be laud and praise.

2
50
mf
laud and praise. A - men.
A1
laud and praise. A - men.
A2
laud and praise. A - men.
laud and praise. A - men.
praise. A - men.

97 WILLIAM BYRD *Christ rising again:* part 1

10
- ing, Christ ris - ing a -
Christ ris - ing a-gain from the dead,
15
- gain from the dead, now di - eth not,
now di - eth not, now di - eth
now di - eth not, di - - - - eth
not, now di - - - eth
etc.

Full
20
not. Death from hence-forth, Death from hence-forth hath
not. Death from hence-forth, Death from hence-forth hath
Death from hence-forth, Death from hence-forth hath no
Death from hence-forth, Death from hence-forth hath
Death from hence-forth, Death from hence-forth hath
Death from hence-forth, Death from hence-forth hath

25
Verse
no pow'r up-on him, for in
no pow'r up-on him, for in that he died,
pow'r up - on him.
no pow'r up - on him.
no pow'r up - on him.
no pow'r up - on him.

30
that he died, he died but once to put a-
he died but once to put a - way sin, to put a-way
[Full] 35
- way sin, to put a-way sin, to put a-way sin,
Full Verse
sin, to put a-way sin, to put a-way sin, but in
[Full]
to put a - way sin, to put a - way sin.
Full
to put a-way sin, to put a-way sin.
Full
to put a-way sin, to put a-way sin.
Full
to put a-way sin, to put a - way sin.
Full Verse

VERSE
but in that he liv - - eth, he
that he liv - - eth, he liv-eth un-to God,
40
liv-eth un-to God, he liv-eth un-to God, un - to God.
he liv-eth un-to God, he liv-eth un-to God.
FULL
45
And so like-wise count your-selves, count your-selves dead un - to
FULL
And so like-wise count your-selves dead, dead un - to
[FULL]
And so like-wise count your-selves, count your-selves dead un - to
[FULL]
And so like-wise count your-selves dead un - - to
FULL
And so like-wise count your-selves dead un - - to sin, dead un - to
FULL

50
sin, but liv - ing, but liv - ing — un - to ——
sin, but liv - ing un - to God, but liv - ing un - to
sin, but liv - ing, but liv - ing un - to
sin, but liv - ing un - to God, but liv - ing un - to
sin, but liv - ing un - to God, un - to

[VERSE]
55
God, in Christ Je - sus our Lord, in Christ
VERSE
God, in Christ Je -
God,
God,
God,
God,
VERSE

Je - sus our Lord,
[Full]
- sus our Lord, in Christ Je - sus our
[Full]
in Christ Je - sus our Lord, in
[Full]
in Christ Je - sus our Lord, in Christ
[Full]
in Christ Je - sus our Lord, our
[Full]
in Christ Je - sus our
Full

60
[Full]
in Christ Je - sus our Lord.
Lord, in Christ Je - sus our Lord.
Christ Je - sus our Lord, Je - sus our Lord.
Je - sus our Lord, Je - sus our Lord.
Lord, Je - sus our Lord.
Lord, in Christ Je - sus our Lord.

98 THOMAS WEELKES *As Vesta was from Latmos hill descending*

 Airs or Fantastic Spirits (1608), ed. Edmund H. Fellowes; rev. Dart. The English Madrigalists, vol. 13.

p
Lat - mos hill, from Lat - mos hill de - scend - - ing, She spied,
- scend - ing, from Lat - mos hill de - - - scend - ing,
p
from Lat - mos hill de - scend - - - ing, She
p
Lat - mos hill de - scend - ing, de - scend - ing, She
p
p
she spied a maid - en Queen the
She spied a maid - en Queen, she spied a maid - en Queen the
spied a maid - en Queen the same a - scend - - - -
spied a maid - en Queen the same a -

cresc.
same a - scend - - - ing, a - scend - - ing, the
cresc.
same a - scend - - - ing, a - scend - ing, the
cresc.
-ing, a - scend - ing, the same a - scend - - - -
cresc.
- scend - - ing, the same a - scend - - - -
cresc.
same a - scend - - ing, the same a - scend - - - ing, At -
same a - scend - - - ing, a - scend - ing,
- ing, a - scend - ing, the same a - scend - - - ing,
- ing, the same a-scend - ing, the same a - scend - ing,
f
f

-tend - ed on by all the shep - - herds swain,
At - tend - ed on by all the shep - herds swain,
At - tend - ed on by all the shep - herds swain,
At - tend - ed on by all the shep - herds swain, at -
At - tend - ed on by all the shep - herds swain,
at - tend - ed on by all the shep - herds swain, To
at - tend - ed on by all the shep - - herds swain,
at - tend - ed on by all the shep - herds swain, To
-tend - ed on by all the shep - herds swain, To
at - tend - ed on by all the shep - herds swain,
At - tend - ed on by all the shep - herds swain, To

whom Di - a - na's dar - lings, dar - - lings Came running
To whom Di - a - na's dir - lings Came run-ning down a-
whom Di - a - na's dar - lings, to whom Di - a - na's dar - - lings
whom Di - a - na's dar - lings Came run-ning down a- main,
To whom Di - a - na's dir - lings
whom Di - a - na's dar - lings Came running down a- main, came
down a- main, came run-ning down a- main,
-main, came run-ning down a - main,
Came run-ning down a - main, came running down a -
a - - - main, came running down a -
Came run-ning down a - main, came running down a - main,
run-ning down a - main, came running down a - main,
cresc.
cresc.
cresc.

cresc.
came run-ning down a - main,
cresc.
came run-ning down a - main,
f
- main, came run-ning down a - main, came run-ning down a -
f
- main, came run-ning down a-main, came
cresc.
came run-ning down a - main, a - main, came
f
cresc.
a - main, came run-ning down a -
f
f
came run-ning down a - main, came run-ning down a - main, came run-ning down a -
f
came run-ning down a - main, came run-ning down a - main, came run-ning down a -
- main, came run - ning
run - ning down a - main, came run - ning
run-ning down a-main, a - main, came
- main, came run - ning

p
- main, a - main, First two by two,
- main, a - main, First two by two, then
down a - main, First two by two,
down a - main, First two by two, then
down a - main,
down a - main, Then
then three by three to - ge - ther, Leav - ing their
three by three to - ge - ther, Leav - ing their
then three by three to - ge - ther, Leav - ing their
three by three to - ge - ther, Leav - ing their
Then three by three to - - ge - ther, Leav - ing their
three by three to - ge - ther, Leav - ing their

God - dess all a - lone hast - ed thi - ther,
mf
God - dess hast - ed thi - ther, And
God - dess hast - ed thi - ther, And
God - dess hast - ed thi - ther,
God - dess hast - ed thi - ther, And
God - dess hast - ed thi - ther,
And min - gling with the shep - herds of her
min - gling with the shep - herds of her train,
min - gling with the shep - herds of her train, of her train,
And min - gling with the shep - herds of her
min - gling with the shep - herds of her train, with the shep - herds of her
And min - gling with the shep - herds of her

train, With mirth - ful tunes, mirth - ful tunes, her pre - sence
With mirth - ful tunes, with mirth-ful tunes, her pre - sence en - ter -
With mirth - ful tunes, with mirth-ful tunes, her pre - sence
train, of her train, With mirth - ful tunes
train,With mirth - ful tunes,with mirth - ful tunes, her pre - sence en - ter -
train, With mirth - ful tunes, her pre - sence en - -
en - ter - tain, her pre - sence en - ter - - tain,
- - - - tain, her pre - sence en - ter - tain,
en - ter - tain, her pre - sence en - ter - tain,
her pre - sence en - - ter - - tain,
- tain, en - ter - - tain, her pre - sence en - ter - tain,
- - ter - tain, her pre - sence en - ter - tain,

ff
mf
Then sang the shep-herds and Nymphs of Di-a - na, Nymphs
Then sang the shep-herds and Nymphs of Di-a - na, Nymphs
Then sang the shep-herds and Nymphs of Di-a - na, Nymphs
Then sang the shep - herds and Nymphs of Di-a - na, Nymphs
Then sang the shep-herds and Nymphs of Di-a - - na,
Then sang the shep-herds and Nymphs of Di-a - na,
f
of Di-a - na, Long live fair O-ri - a-na, fair
of Di-a - na, Long live fair O-ri-a-na,
of Di-a - na, of Di - a - - -
of Di-a - na, Long live fair
Long live fair O-ri-a-na, Long live
Long live fair O-ri -

f
sf
O - ri - a - na, Long live fair O - ri - a - na, Long
O - ri - a - na, Long live fair O - ri - a -
-na, Long live fair O - ri - a - na, Long live fair
O - ri - a - na, Long live fair O - ri - a - na,
fair O - ri - a - na, Long live fair O - ri -
-a - na, Long
sf
live fair O - ri - a - na, Long live fair O - ri - a - na,
-na, Long live fair O - ri - a - na, Long
O - ri - a - na, Long live fair O - ri - a - na, fair
Long live fair O - ri - a - na, fair O - ri -
-a - na, fair O - ri - a - na, Long live fair O - ri -
live

O - ri-a - na, Long live fair O - ri - a - na, Long
live fair O - ri - a - na, Long live fair O - ri -
O - ri - a - na, Long live fair O - ri - a -
-a - na, Long live fair O - ri - a - na, Live long, long live fair
-a - na, Long live fair O - ri - a - na,
fair O - ri -
live fair O - ri - a - na, fair O - ri - a - na, Long
-a - na, Long live fair O - ri - a - na, Long live fair
-na, Long live fair O - ri - a - na,
O - ri - a - na, fair O - ri - a -
fair O - ri - a - na, Long live fair O - ri -
a - na,

live fair O - ri - a - na, fair O - ri - a - na, Long
O - ri - a - na, O - ri - a - - na, Long live fair O - ri -
Long live fair O - ri - a - - na, fair O - - -
-na, Long live fair O - ri - a - - - - na,
-a - na, Long live fair O - ri - a - na, Long live fair
live fair O - ri - a - na, fair O - ri - a - - na, fair
-a - na, Long live fair O - ri - a - na, fair O - ri -
- ri - a - na, Long live fair O - ri - a - na,
Long live fair O - ri - a - na, Long
O - ri - a - na, Long live fair O - ri - a - na,
ff
Long live fair O - - ri -

O - ri - a - na, Long live fair O - ri - a - na,
-a - na, Long live fair O - ri - a - na, Long live fair O - ri -
O - ri - a - - na, Long
live fair O - ri - a - na, Long live fair O - ri - a -
Long live fair O - - ri - a - -
-a - - na, Long live fair O - ri - a - na, fair
Long live fair O - ri - a - - - - na.
-a - na, Long live fair O - ri - a - na.
live fair O - ri - a - na, fair O - ri - a - na.
-na, fair O - ri - a - na.
-na, Long live fair O - ri - a - - na.
O - - - ri - a - - na.

99a GIOVANNI GIACOMO GASTOLDI *A lieta vita*

 Le pupitre, vol. 10 (Paris, 1968)

15
la la la. Chi gio - ir bra - ma, Se di cor
la la la, Chi gio - ir bra - ma, Se di cor
la la la la, Chi gio - ir bra - ma, Se di cor
la la la. Chi gio - ir bra - ma, Se di cor
la la la, Chi gio - ir bra - ma, Se di cor
20
a - ma, Do - ne - rà il co - re, A un tal Si - gno - re,
a - ma, Do - ne - rà il co - re, A un tal Si - gno - re,
a - ma, Do - ne - rà il co - re, A un tal Si - gno - re,
a - ma, Do - ne - rà il co - re, A un tal Si - gno - re,
a - ma, Do - ne - rà il co - re, A un tal Si - gno - re,
25
Fa la la la la la la la la la. Chi gio - ir
Fa la la la la la la la la la. Chi gio - ir
Fa la la la la la la la la, Chi gio - ir
Fa la la la la la la la la. Chi gio - ir
Fa la la la la la la la la. Chi gio - ir

Hor lieta homai
Scacciando i guai, Fa la la
Quanto ci resta
Viviamo in festa
E diam l'honore
A un tal Signore, Fa la la

Chi a lui non crede
Privo è di fede, Fa la la
Onde haver merta
Contra se aperta
L'ira e'l furore
D'un tal Signore, Fa la la

Ne fuggir giova
Ch'egli ognun trova, Fa la la
Veloci ha l'ali
E foco e strali
Dunque s'adore
Un tal Signore, Fa la la.

99b THOMAS MORLEY *Sing we and chant it*

First Book of Balletts (1595/1600), ed. Edmund H. Fellowes; rev. Dart. The English Madrigalists, vol. 4. © 1913, 1965 by Stainer & Bell Ltd. Used by permission.

p
cresc.
f
1. Not long youth last - eth, and old age hast - eth, Now is best lei - sure, To take our plea-sure.
2. Hence care be pack - ing, No mirth be lack - ing, Let spare no trea - sure, To live in plea-sure.
1. Not long youth last - eth, and old age hast - eth, Now is best lei-sure, To take our plea-sure.
2. Hence care be pack - ing, No mirth be lack - ing, Let spare no trea-sure, To live in plea-sure.
1. Not long youth last - eth, and old age hast - eth, Now is best lei - sure, To take our plea-sure.
2. Hence care be pack - ing, No mirth be lack - ing, Let spare no trea - sure, To live in plea-sure.
1. Not long youth last - eth, and old age hast - eth, Now is best lei-sure, To take our plea-sure.
2. Hence care be pack - ing, No mirth be lack - ing, Let spare no trea-sure, To live in plea-sure.
1. Not long youth last - eth, and old age hast - eth, Now is best lei - sure, To take our plea-sure.
2. Hence care be pack - ing, No mirth be lack - ing, Let spare no trea - sure, To live in plea-sure.
1.
2.
Fa la la la la la. Fa la la la la. la.
Fa la la la la la la la la. Fa la la la. Fa la la la. la.
Fa la la la. Fa la la la la la la la. Fa la la la la. la.
Fa la la la la la. Fa la la la la la la la. Fa la la la la. la.
Fa la la la la la la la. Fa la la la la la la la — la. la.

100 JOHN DOWLAND *In darkness let me dwell*

all cheer-ful light from me, The walls of mar - ble
black that mois - tened, that mois - tened still shall
weep, still shall weep, My mu - sic, my mu - sic
hell - ish, hell - ish jar - ring sounds, jar - ring, jarring

sounds, to ——— ba - nish, ba-nish friend - ly sleep.
Thus wed - ded to my woes, And bed - ded
to my tomb, O, let me, liv-ing, die,
O, let me, living, let me, liv - ing, living, die, Till death, till death do come,

till death, till death do come, till death, till death do come,
In dark - ness let me dwell.

101 WILLIAM BYRD *Browning my dear*

1.
"The leaves be greene, the nuttes be browne, thay hange soe highe thay
will not come downe."
2.
3.

25
4.
30
35
5.
40
6.
45

50
7.
55
8.
60
65
9.

70
10.
75
80
11.
85
12.

90
95
13.
100
105
14.
110

115
15.
120
16.
125

130
17.
135
18.
140

145
19.
150
20.
155
160

102 JOHN BULL *Walsingham*

3.
4.
5.

6.
7.

8.
9.

(♮)
(♯)
10.

11.
12.

13.

14.
(♯)
(♯) (♯)
(♯)
(♯)
(♯)
15.

16.

17.
18.

(♯)
(♯)
19.

20.
21.

22.

23.
24.

(♯)
(♯)(♯)
25.

26.
(♯) (♯)
(♯) (♯) (♯) (♯)
27.

28.

29.
30.

Translations

The Ordinary of the Mass
(for Nos. 16, 17, 18b, 19, 21, 24, 25b, 41, 42, 44, 62, 85)

Kyrie eleison.
Christe eleison.
Kyrie eleison.

Lord have mercy.
Christ have mercy.
Lord have mercy.

Gloria in excelsis Deo. Et in terra pax hominibus bonae voluntatis. Laudamus te. Benedicimus te. Adoramus te. Glorificamus te. Gratias agimus tibi propter magnam gloriam tuam. Domine Deus, Rex caelestis, Deus Pater omnipotens. Domine Fili unigenite Jesu Christe. Domine Deus, Agnus Dei, Filius Patris. Qui tollis peccata mundi, miserere nobis. Qui tollis peccata mundi, suscipe deprecationem nostram. Qui sedes dexteram Patris, miserere nobis. Quoniam tu solus sanctus. Tu solus Dominus. Tu solus Altissimus, Jesu Christe. Cum Sancto Spiritu, in gloria Dei Patris. Amen

Glory to God in the highest. And on earth peace to men of good will. We praise thee, we bless thee, we adore thee, we glorify thee. We give thee thanks for thy great glory. O Lord God, King of heaven, God the Father almighty. O Lord, the only begotten Son, Jesus Christ. O Lord God, Lamb of God, Son of the Father. Thou who takest away the sins of the world, have mercy upon us. Thou who takest away the sins of the world, receive our prayer. Thou who sittest at the right hand of the Father, have mercy upon us. For thou only art holy, thou only art Lord, thou only art most high, O Jesus Christ, with the Holy Ghost, in the glory of God the Father. Amen.

Credo in unum Deum. Patrem omnipotentem, factorem caeli et terrae, visibilium omnium, et invisibilium. Et in unum Dominum Jesum Christum, Filium Dei unigenitum. Et ex Patre natum ante omnia saecula. Deum de Deo, lumen de lumine, Deum verum de Deo vero. Genitum, non factum, consubstantialem Patri: per quem omnia facta sunt. Qui propter nos homines, et propter nostram salutem descendit de caelis. Et incarnatus est de Spiritu Sancto ex Maria Virgine: Et homo factus est. Crucifixus etiam pro nobis: sub Pontio Pilato passus, et sepultus est. Et resurrexit tertia die, secundum Scripturas. Et ascendit in caelum: sedet ad dexteram Patris. Et iterum venturus est cum gloria judicare vivos et mortuos: cujus regni non erit finis. Et in Spiritum Sanctum, Dominum, et vivificantem: qui ex Patre Filioque procedit. Qui cum Patre et Filio simul adoratur et conglorificatur: qui locutus est per Prophetas. Et unam sanctam catholicam et apostolicam Ecclesiam. Confiteor unum baptisma in remissionem peccatorum. Et exspecto resurrectionem mortuorum. Et vitam venturi saeculi. Amen.

I believe in one God, Father almighty, maker of heaven and earth and of all things visible and invisible. And in one Lord Jesus Christ, the only begotten Son of God, born of the Father before all ages. God of God, light of light, true God of true God. Begotten, not made, being of one substance with the Father, by whom all things were made. Who for us men and for our salvation came down from heaven. And was made incarnate by the Holy Ghost of the Virgin Mary, and was made man. And was crucified for us under Pontius Pilate. He suffered and was buried. And the third day he rose again according to the Scriptures. And ascended into heaven, and sitteth on the right hand of the Father. And he shall come again with glory to judge the living and the dead; of whose kingdom there shall be no end. And in the Holy Ghost, Lord and giver of life, who proceedeth from the Father and the Son. Who, together with the Father and the Son, is worshipped and glorified; who spake by the prophets. And one holy, Catholic, and Apostolic Church. I acknowledge one baptism for the remission of sins. And I look for the resurrection of the dead, and the life of the world to come. Amen.

Sanctus, Sanctus, Sanctus Dominus Deus Sabaoth. Pleni sunt caeli et terra gloria tua. Hosanna in excelsis. Benedictus qui venit in nomine Domine. Hosanna in excelsis.

Holy, holy, holy, Lord God of Hosts. The heavens and earth are full of thy glory. Hosanna in the highest. Blessed is he who comes in the name of the Lord. Hosanna in the highest.

Agnus Dei, qui tollis peccata mundi: miserere nobis. Agnus Dei, qui tollis peccata mundi: miserere nobis. Agnus Dei, qui tollis peccata mundi: dona nobis pacem.

Lamb of God, who takest away the sins of the world, have mercy upon us. Lamb of God, who takest away the sins of the world, have mercy upon us. Lamb of God, who takest away the sins of the world, grant us peace.

1. Dunstable, *Quam pulchra es*

How lovely and wonderful you are, most beloved, in your delights. Your stature is like a palm tree, and your breasts like grapes. Your head is like Mount Carmel, your neck like an ivory tower. Come, my love, let us go into the fields, and see if the flowers bear fruit and the pomegranates bud. There will I give you my love. Alleluia.

2. Brassart, *Sapienciam sanctoram*

[Antiphon] The populace relates the wisdom of the saints, and the gathering announces their praises: their name lives on forever. [Psalm verse] Exult, you just, in the Lord: praise from the upright is fitting. [Lesser Doxology] Glory be to the Father, and to the Son, and to the Holy Ghost. As it was in the beginning, is now and ever shall be, world without end. Amen.

3. Du Fay, *Ave regina caelorum*

Hail, queen of heaven, hail, mistress of the angels; hail, holy source, from whom the light of the world comes forth; rejoice, glorious one, beautiful above all; farewell, in your perfection, and pray to Christ for us forever.

4. Dunstable, *Veni sancte spiritus / Veni creator*

Top voice: Come, Holy Ghost, and from heaven shine the ray of your light. Come, Father of the poor; come, provider of gifts; come, light of hearts. Greatest comforter, sweet guest of the soul, sweet refreshment. Repose in work, coolness in heat, solace in tears. O most blessed light, fill the innermost hearts of your faithful. Without your divinity there is no light, nothing is harmless. Wash what is impure, irrigate what is parched, heal what is diseased. Flex what is rigid, melt what is frozen, straighten what is bent. Give to your faithful who confide in you your sevenfold sacred gift. Give them virtue's reward, grant salvation after death, grant eternal glory.

Second voice: Come, Holy Ghost, and pour upon us the dew of heaven's grace. Save us, who pray as humans with your divinity, from the serpent in whose presence, through your clemency, our sins are hidden, and make our obedient, penitent hearts pleasing to you. Comforter of the languished and restorer of the strayed, curer of death, forgiver of sinners, be our defender, and guide [us] to the divine.

Third voice: Come, Creator Spirit, visit the minds of your own, fill with heavenly grace those hearts that you have created. Called Paraclete, gift of the highest God, living fount, flame, love, and the anointing of the spirit. You are sevenfold in your munificence, you are the finger of God's right hand; in the Father's promise, you give voice to throats. Kindle light in the senses, fill hearts with love, firm our weak bodies with virtue forever. Drive the enemy into the distance, grant peace quickly. With you therefore leading, we forestall all harm. Through you we learn of the Father and also know the Son; in you, through both forms of the Spirit, we believe forever.

Tenor: Visit the minds of your own, fill with heavenly grace.

5. Anonymous, *Deo gracias, Anglia*

Opening burden: Give thanks to God, O England, for the victory.
Subsequent burdens: Thanks be to God.

6. Grenon, *La plus jolie et la plus belle*

The happiest and the most beautiful, the most cheerful, the freshest, graced most agreeably with sweetness, it is she in whom, day in and day out, my heart joyfully renews itself.

7. Baude Cordier, *Se cuer d'amant*

This lover's heart brought low by her
can render favor as well as contempt.
It seems to me that my esteemed lady
ought to release me from my woes.

My heart does nothing except grieve,
but nonetheless it cannot be mended.
  This lover's heart . . .

Since those who are most important and most learned
see me play the fool at any time
(seeing that I need only a little incentive),
I can well say to them without misleading,
  This lover's heart . . .

(Trans. Honey Meconi)

8. Ciconia, *Ut te per omnes / Ingens alumnus Padue*

Top voice: Enlighten our unclean spirits, [Saint] Francis, that we may follow thee with full reverence through all trials that come from on high. Thou that watches over the seats of eternal glory of the Father, who shakes all things with a single nod, protect us from evil. Through the wound of Christ, which he freely accepted and which thou didst also receive, kindly grant us that the fortunate Order of Friars Minor, which thou didst found and that sings thy praises, may last forever. Amen.

Second voice: Francesco, the famous offspring of Padua, Zabarella by name, worshipping the power of kindly [Saint] Francis beseeches him: Be a well-disposed protector for thy servant that prays to thee, whom the whole world acclaims with outstanding honors and with songs. Holy Francis, freely hear the worthy prayer of this great teacher, from whom Antenor's line receives good laws. Come thou leader of the faithful, raised in the deep forests, enclosed in a mighty body, and guiding the way of the heavenly. Amen.

(*The Works of Ciconia*, Polyphonic Music of the Fourteenth Century 24, ed. Margaret Bent and Anne Hallmark [Monaco: L'Oiseau-Lyre, 1985], 224–25)

9. Ciconia, *O rosa bella*
10. Dunstable/Bedyngham, *O rosa bella*

O beautiful rose, o my sweet soul,
don't let me die, for the sake of kindness.

  Alas, must I end sorrowfully
  because I served well and loved loyally?

  Help me now in my pining,
  heart of my heart, don't let me suffer.

O god of love, how painful is this love!
See that I die every hour because of this thought.

O beautiful rose . . .

11. Du Fay, *Resvellies vous*

Awake and be merry,
all lovers who love nobility;
enjoy yourselves, flee melancholy;
do not tire of serving well,
for today will be the wedding,
with great honor and noble company;
it is necessary for each of you to celebrate
and join the happy company.
    Noble Charles, who is named Malatesta.

He has chosen a lady, beautiful and good,
by whom he will be greatly honored,
because she comes from a very noble line
of barons who are much renowned;
her own name is Victoria,
and she is the offspring of the Colonna;
it is right, then, that he requests
to have a good life with this lady.
    Noble Charles, who is named Malatesta.

12. Du Fay, *Adieu, m'amour*

Farewell, my love, farewell, my joy,
farewell, the solace that I had,
farewell, my loyal mistress.
Saying farewell so deeply wounds me
that it seems to me that I must die.

From grief I weep exceedingly.
There is no comfort that I see,
when I leave you, my princess.

    Farewell, my love . . .

I pray to God that He may go with me,
and grant that I soon again see you,
my treasure, my love, and my goddess.
For it seems to me, about what I leave,
that after my pain I should have joy.

    Farewell, my love . . .

(Don M. Randel, "Dufay the Reader," *Studies in the History of Music,*
vol. 1: *Music and Language* [New York: Broude Bros., 1983]: 42–43)

13. Binchois, *Dueil angoisseus*

Anguished grief, immoderate fury, grievous despair, full of madness, endless languor and a life of misfortune, full of tears, anguish, and torment, doleful heart, living in darkness, wraithlike body on the point of death, are mine continually without cease; and thus I can neither be cured nor die. Harsh disdain, bereft of joy, sad thoughts, deep sighs, great anguish locked in a weary heart, bitter distress endured in secret, mournful demeanor without gladness, foreboding which dries up all hope, are in me and never leave me; and thus . . . Worry and annoy everlasting, bitter waking, troubled sleep, labor in vain, with languid expression, destined to grievous torment, and all the ill that one could ever say or think, without hope of relief, torment me immoderately; and thus . . . Prince, pray to God that very soon

He may grant me death, if He does not wish by any other means to remedy the ill in which I painfully languish; and thus. . .

(Translation by Stephen Haynes, in record notes for Christopher Page,
The Castle of Fair Welcome, Hyperion A66194 [1986]. Reproduced by
courtesy of Hyperion Records, London.)

14. Du Fay, *Nuper rosarum flores*

1. The harsh winter [of the Hebraic Law] having past, roses, a recent papal gift, perpetually adorn the Temple of the grandest structure piously and devoutly dedicated to you, heavenly Virgin.

2. Today the vicar of Jesus Christ and successor of Peter, Eugenius, this same most enormous Temple with sacred hands and holy oils, has deigned to consecrate.

3. Therefore, sweet parent and daughter of your son, God, virgin of virgins, to you your devoted populace of Florence petitions that whoever begs for something with pure spirit and body,

4. Through your intercession and the merits of your son, their lord, owing to his carnal torment, it may be worthy to receive gracious benefits and forgiveness of sins. Amen.

Tenors I-II: Awesome is this place.

(Craig Wright, "Dufay's *Nuper rosarum flores,* King Solomon's
Temple, and the Veneration of the Virgin," *Journal of the
American Musicological Society* 47 [1994]: 399. All rights reserved.)

15. Du Fay, *Ave regina caelorum* (III)

(The lines in italics are Du Fay's tropes.)
Hail, queen of heaven, hail, mistress of the angels. *Have mercy on your dying Dufay, or, as a sinner, he will be cast down into the fires of hell.* Hail, holy source, from whom the light of the world comes forth. *Have mercy, Mother of God, so that the gate of heaven is open to the weak.* Rejoice, glorious one, beautiful above all. *Have mercy on your supplicant Dufay, and may you see beauty in his death.* Farewell, in your perfection, and pray to Christ for us forever. *Have mercy on us, so that we are not damned on high; and help us at the hour of death, so that we feel peace in our hearts.*

18a. Du Fay, *Se la face ay pale*

If my face is pale, love is the cause; that is the principal reason. And to love is so bitter for me that I could drown myself in the sea. Now, she knows well, that lady whom I serve, that I can have no happiness or live without her.

If I carry a heavy burden of sorrow, it is because this love is hard for me to bear, because she will not cease being cruel to anyone who does not obey her; and such is her power, that I cannot live without her.

She is the most regal woman that anyone could ever see. I cannot resist loving her loyally, though I am a fool to look upon her and wish not to find love elsewhere. I believe that, even without wishing to suffer, I cannot live without her.

20. Binchois, *Magnificat tercii toni*

My soul doth magnify the Lord, and my spirit hath rejoiced in God my Savior. For He hath regarded the low estate of His handmaiden: for, behold, from henceforth all generations shall call me blessed. For He that is mighty hath done to me great things; and holy is His name. And His mercy is on them that fear Him from generation to generation. He hath shown strength with His arm; He hath scattered the proud in the imagination of their hearts. He hath put down the mighty from their seats, and exalted them of low degree. He hath filled the hungry with good things; and the rich He hath sent empty away. He hath helped His servant Israel, in remembrance of His mercy; as He spake to our fathers, to Abraham, and to his seed forever. Glory be to the Father, and to the Son, and to the Holy Ghost. As it was in the beginning, is now and ever shall be, world without end. Amen.

22. Morton, *Il sera pour vous / L'homme armé*

Superius:
He will be engaged in combat by you,
the dreaded Turk, Master Symon.
Certainly, that will be for sure,
and he'll be struck down by the point of the axe.

    His pride we hold humbled,
    If he falls into your hands, the villain.

      He will be engaged. . .

In a short time you will have beaten him,
If it pleases God; men shall then be able to say:
Long live Symonet the Breton,
For he has fought the Turk.

      He will be engaged. . .

Tenor:
The armed man, the armed man is to be feared, the armed man. The cry has been heard everywhere, "To the assault." Let everyone arm himself with a coat of iron mail. The armed man, the armed man is to be feared.

Contratenor:
The armed man, the armed man is to be feared, the armed man. To the assault, let everyone arm himself. To the assault. The armed man, the armed man is to be feared.

(*Robert Morton: The Collected Works*, Masters and Monuments of Renaissance Music 2, ed. Allan Atlas [New York: Broude Bros., 1981], 69–70)

23. Busnoys, *In hydraulis*

Pythagoras, in former times, admiring the melodies of water organs, and the sounds of hammers on struck surfaces, by the inequalities of their weights, discovered the natures of the Muses. Epitrite and hemiola, epogdoon and duple produce the concord of fourth and fifth, the tone and the octave, while they draw together the species of the monochord.

You, Ockeghem, who sing these harmonies before all in the hall of the king of the French, strengthen the practice of your progeny, as you perceive it on occasion in the halls of the Duke of Burgundy in your homeland. Through me, Busnoys, unworthy musician of the illustrious Count of Charolais, may you be greeted according to your merits as the supreme head of melody; hail, true image of Orpheus!

(Leeman Perkins, in *Antoine Busnoys: Collected Works*, vol. 3: *The Latin-Texted Works*, Masters and Monuments of Renaissance Music 5, ed. Richard Taruskin [New York: The Broude Trust, 1990], 75)

25a. Ockeghem, *Fors seulement*

Save only the expectation that I shall die,
no hope dwells in my weary heart,
for my misery torments me so severely
that there is no sorrow I do not feel because of you,
since I am very sure of losing you.

    Your severity pursues me to such a degree
    that I must in this regard assure myself
    I have nothing at all with which to be content

      save only the expectation that I shall die.

    All alone I bemoan my distress,
    cursing, by my oath, at all times
    my faithfulness which has made me so unhappy.
    Alas, I am sorry to be alive,
    since because of you I have nothing left to me

      save only the expectation that I shall die.

(*Johannes Ockeghem: Collected Works* 3, ed. Richard Wexler [American Musicological Society, 1992], lxiv–lxv. All rights reserved.)

26. Regis, *Clangat plebs flores*

The text is terribly convoluted and at times corrupt. It may be summarized as follows: the populace is asked to sing songs that praise the Virgin Mary so that they might overcome her enemies and resist sin.

27. Busnoys, *Je ne puis vivre*

I cannot live like this forever
unless I have, in my misery,
some comfort;
only an hour—or less, or more,
and every day
I will serve you loyally, Love,
until death.

    Lady, noble in name and arms,
    I have written this song for you,

    Weeping warm tears from my eyes
    in order that you have mercy upon me.

As for me, I die slowly but surely,
awake at night, walking back and forth a hundred times,
crying loudly:
"Vengence," to God, because most unfairly,
I'm drowning in tears;
just when I need help, I get none,
and Pity: sleeps!

I cannot live like this forever . . .

28. Ockeghem, *S'elle m'amera / Petite camusette*

If she will love me I don't know,
but I'll try

to win something of her favor.
I'm forced to go that way;
this time I'll give it a try.

The other day, I advanced so far
that I nearly let my heart
go, without having asked her

if she will love me . . .

Then, after it was over, I thought
that I had not stopped for a long time;
it was not that I did not love her,
but it's a game of hocus-pocus:
I am just as I began.

If she will love me . . .

Lower voices: Little pugnose, you have placed me close to death. Robin and Marion are going to the woods, they go arm in arm; they have fallen asleep. Little pugnose, you have placed me close to death.

29. Hayne van Ghizeghem, *De tous biens plaine*

My mistress has every virtue,
everyone owes her honorable tribute,
for she is as possessed of worth
as was ever any goddess.

On seeing her, I am so happy
that my heart turns into paradise.

My mistress has every virtue. . .

I desire no other riches
except to be her servant;
and since there is no better choice,
my motto will always be:

My mistress has every virtue. . .

31. Anonymous, *Mein herz in steten trewen*

My heart has been constantly faithful in hope toward you; she who increases my joy more and more with each passing day. Her love has embraced me, to which end I betake myself; my yearning is ever toward her; my distress would pass if she treated me sweetly.

32. Cornago, *¿Qu'es mi vida preguntays?*

What is my life, do you ask?
I do not wish to deny it to you;
to love well and to lament
is the life that you give me.

Who could have served you
as well as I have served you?

My troubled life,
who could have suffered [it]?

Why me, do you ask?
I want to get over this grief,
for to love well and to lament
is the life that I give you.

(*Johannes Cornago: Complete Works*, Recent Researches in the Music of the Middle Ages and Early Renaissance 15, ed. Rebecca Gerber [Madison: A-R Editions, 1984], xxv–xxvi)

33. Serafino dall'Aquila, *Sufferir son disposto*

I am disposed to suffer every torment,
torment where there is no repose.

Repose would make me content,
content from the love hidden within me.

I feel a hidden fire in my breast,
I feel my sorrowful heart consumes me.

I live in sorrow and consent to my unhappiness.
I consent to die, o glorious one.

34. Robert Morton, *Le souvenir*

The memory of you kills me,
my only love, when I do not see you,
because I swear to you upon my faith,
without you my happiness is lost.

When you are out of my sight,
I lament and say to myself:

The memory of you . . .

Alone I remain deprived,
I receive no comfort from anyone,
and thus suffer without display
until your return.

The memory of you . . .

(*Robert Morton: The Collected Works*, Masters and Monuments of Renaissance Music 2, ed. Allan Atlas [New York: Broude Bros., 1981], 75–76)

37. Josquin, *Ave Maria . . . virgo serena*

Hail Mary, queen of grace,
Lord be with you, serene virgin.

Hail to her whose conception,
full of solemn jubilation,
fills heaven and earth
with new joy.

Hail to her whose birth
brought us solemnity,
as the light of the morning star
anticipates the true sun.

Hail, pious humility,
fruitful without a man,
whose annunciation
brought us salvation.

Hail, true virginity,
immaculate chastity,
whose purification
cleansed our sins.

Hail, remarkable one in all
angelic virtues,
whose assumption
was our glorification.

Mother of God, remember us. Amen.

38. Isaac, *Quis dabit capiti meo aquam?*

Who will send water to my head? Who will fill the fount of tears for my eyes, that I may weep by night, that I may weep by day? Thus the widowed turtle dove, thus the dying swan, thus the nightingale is overcome. Alas, poor sufferer! Such grief! The laurel is stricken down suddenly by the lightning bolt, the laurel celebrated by the choirs of all the muses and nymphs, beneath whose canopy Phoebus's lyre sounds mellower and voice sweeter; now all are mute, all silent.

(Trans. Frederick Purnell)

39. Josquin(?)/La Rue(?), *Absalon, fili mi*

Absalon, my son, would that I would die for thee, my son Absalon. Let me live no longer, but descend into hell weeping.

40. Josquin, *Miserere mei, Deus*

1. Have mercy upon me, O God, according to thy loving kindness:
2. According unto the multitude of thy tender mercies blot out my transgressions. [Verses 1-2 = a single verse in the Protestant-Jewish tradition.]
3. Wash me thoroughly from mine iniquity and cleanse me from my sin.
4. For I acknowledge my transgressions: and my sin is ever before me.
5. Against thee, thee only, have I sinned, and done this evil in thy sight: that thou mightest be justified when thou speakest, and be clear when thou judgest.
6. Behold, I was shapen in iniquity: and in sin did my mother conceive me.
7. Behold, thou desirest truth in the inward parts: and in the hidden part thou shalt make me to know wisdom.
8. Purge me with hyssop, and I shall be clean: wash me, and I shall be whiter than snow.
9. Make me to hear joy and gladness: that the bones which thou hast broken may rejoice.
10. Hide thy face from my sins, and blot out all mine iniquities.
11. Create in me a clean heart, O God: and renew a right spirit within me.
12. Cast me not away from thy presence: and take not thy holy spirit from me.
13. Restore unto me the joy of thy salvation, and uphold me with thy free spirit.
14. Then will I teach transgressors thy ways: and sinners shall be converted unto thee.
15. Deliver me from blood guiltiness, O God, thou God of my salvation: and my tongue shall sing aloud of thy righteousness.
16. O Lord, open thou my lips: and my mouth shall show forth thy praise.
17. For thou desirest not sacrifice; else would I give it: thou delightest not in burnt offering.
18. The sacrifices of God are a broken spirit: a broken and a contrite heart, O God, thou wilt not despise.
19. Do good in thy good pleasure unto Zion: build thou the walls of Jerusalem.
20. Then shalt thou be pleased with the sacrifices of righteousness, with burnt offering and whole burnt offering: then shall they offer bullocks upon thine altar.

43. La Rue, *Missa pro defunctis*: Introit

Eternal rest grant unto them, O Lord: and let perpetual light shine upon them. To you we owe our hymn of praise, O God, in Sion; to you must vows be fulfilled in Jerusalem. Hear my prayer; to you all flesh must come. Eternal rest . . .

45. Compère, *Venes, regretz*

Come, sorrows, come, it is time,
come, make your dwelling with me,
there is good reason for me to implore you;
for today all my joy is dead,
and there is nothing that comes to the rescue.

To this end—that my heart feels and weeps
the hurt it has taken and against which it labors—
I am constrained to open the great door to you.

Come, sorrows, come. . .

But take care that you do not dwell with
the habit of mourning, darker than the lovely mulberry
full of tears, because I must wear them;
delay no more, for my consciousness leaves me,
if you wish to see me before I die,

come, sorrows, come. . .

(Trans. Susan Jackson)

46. Josquin, *Plus nulz regretz*

1. No more discontent, neither large, medium, nor small,
2. of such joy nothing can be spoken or written,
3. now has arrived the happy age of Saturn,
4. where complaints and cries are little known.
5. For so long we have had unlimited sadness,
6. from battles, strife, plundering, and famine.
7. But now we are strengthened with hope,
8. joined and united we have no more discontent.
9. On our fields and green gardens
10. the lyre of Apollo will shine with its noble rays.
11. And so will grow to maturity the shoots of our beards
12. without any abuse or troublesome perils.
13. Discontent no more will come to us afterward.
14. Our time is near, coming from celestial blessings.
15. Let it go elsewhere, this discontent, harder than stone,
16. haughty and harsh, and seek out other nests,
17. if Mars takes from us the white fleur-de-lis,
18. without any offense, and if Venus gives to us

19. the amorous vermilion rose of great price,
20. with which our spirits will have discontent no more.

(Christopher Reynolds, "Musical Evidence of Compositional Planning in the Renaissance: Josquin's *Plus nulz regretz*," *Journal of the American Musicological Society* 40 [1987]: 56.)

47. La Rue, *Pourquoy non*

Why not, why may I not die?
Why not, why may I not fetch
the end of my sad life,
when I love her who does not love me
and serve without gaining favor?

48. Ninot le Petit, *Et la la la*

La la la, treat her well.

I got up one morning, the fresh morning.
I went into the garden to pick clove.

La la la, treat her well, the pretty shepherdess.

I entered our garden to pick clove.
There I found my love, who had picked it.

La la la, treat her well, the pretty shepherdess.

49. Josquin, *Baisés moy*

[Boy] "Kiss me, kiss me! Kiss me, my sweet friend, I pray to you for love."
[Girl] "Don't do it."
[Boy] "And why not?"
[Girl] "If I messed around, my mom would marry me off."
[Boy?/Girl?/Both?] "That's it!"

50. Josquin, *Faulte d'argent*

Lack of money is sorrow unequaled.
If I say this, alas, I well know why.
Without money, one must remain silent.
A woman who sleeps will awaken for money.

(Lawrence F. Bernstein, "A Canonic Chanson in a German Manuscript," in *Von Isaac bis Bach—Studien zur älteren deutschen Musikgeschichte: Festschrift Martin Just zum 60. Geburtstag* [Kassel: Bärenreiter, 1991], 60. Used by kind permission of Bärenreiter-Verlag.)

51. Cara, *Ala absentia*

For the absence that breaks my heart
I find no other consolation,
only the faith that my lady
has promised me, whether I live or die.

She promised, and I swore
to love others no more,
so that no woman in the world
could ever make me leave her,
she who makes the spirit live at all times,
times that wrongfully seem so far away.
Only the faith . . .

(Trans. Carolina Carry)

52. Coppini, *Canto di zingane*

Give some charity to us wretched, hopeless and roaming. We are gypsies, as you can see, emaciated from the great force of rain and snow; to live with you we came, with these children in our arms, wretched us. From far away countries and odd places, tired, we came little by little, just to offer you delight, festivity, and games, if you will be charitable to us wretched. We have among us some who are so skilled in working with their hands and are so ingenious that no one else can equal us; thus have pity on us wretched. You will hear good fortune from us if you will put yours over ours, your graceful hand, I mean; you will hear about your life from beginning to end. We are used to playing and dancing all the time with whoever among you would like it; one more game shall we play: "what is in and what is out," that sweet pleasure brings at the end. However, dear ladies, open the doors, which you keep closed, tight and shut, before death overtakes you, take pleasure in us, poor wretched.

(Trans. Carolina Carry)

53. Josquin, *El grillo*

The cricket is a good singer who holds a long verse [note]. Go ahead, cricket, drink and sing. But he's not like the other birds, who sing a little and then go on to another place. The cricket always stands firm. When it's hottest, he sings for love alone.

54. Escobar, *Passame por Dios barquero*

Boatman, steer me, for the love of God,
to that shore of the river.
Have pity on my love.

For if you delay
in coming to my aid,

you will be of no help to me
as my passion grows.

Do not ask for my perdition,
for I confide in your goodness.
Have pity on my love.

55. Juan del Encina, *Una sañosa porfía*

A bloody struggle is being waged without hope. From then on I never had happiness. My doom is already ordained. Now fortune has disposed to take away my happy command. That brave lion of Spain comes threatening me with evil. He's routing my Moors, razing the fields, as my troops and chieftains he comes conquering. A generous Virgin comes giving them strength. A famous knight comes flying before them, with a red cross and a shining sword, dressed in a sumptuous mantle, leading all the troops.

(Trans. William Sherzer)

56. Finck, *Ich stund an einem morgen*

I stood one morning concealed in a secret hiding place, I heard pitiful words from a pretty and elegant young girl; she said to her lover that they must separate.

57. Isaac, *Innsbruck, ich muss dich lassen*

Innsbruck, I must leave you, I am going on my way into a foreign land. My joy is taken from me, I know not how to regain it while in such misery. I must now endure great pain, which I confide only to my dearest love. O beloved, find pity in your heart for me, poor soul, that I must part from you. My comfort above all other women, I shall always be yours, forever faithful, in honor true. May the good Lord protect you and keep you in your virtue for me, till I return.

(Trans. Noah Greenberg and Paul Maynard, in *Norton Anthology of Western Music*, vol. 1 [New York: Norton, 1980], 234)

61. Gombert, *Quem dicunt homines*

"Whom do people say the Son of Man is?" [asked Jesus]. Peter responded, saying to him: "You are Christ, son of the living God." And Jesus answered and said: "Blessed are you, Simon Baronia: for flesh and blood has not revealed it to you, but my Father, who is in heaven. And I say to you: you are Peter, and upon this rock I will build my Church."

"Peter, do you love me?" He answered, saying: "You know, Lord, for I love you and I devote my spirit to you." And Jesus said: "Lead my disciples. I have prayed for you, and your faith has not failed; and when you are converted, strengthen your brothers." Alleluia.

63. Claudin de Sermisy, *Je n'ay point plus d'affection*

I no longer have any feelings,
except for those I wish to have;
and thus I have no passion,
if I do not wish to have such.
I have gained such power over myself,
such credit and authority,
that whatever I command to my own power,
fragility cannot overcome.

(Trans. Susan Jackson)

64. Passereau, *Il est bel et bon*

Cousin, my husband is handsome and good.

There were two country women
saying one to the other: have you a good husband?

Cousin . . .

He doesn't get angry at me, nor does he hit me,
he does the chores, he feeds the chickens,
and I take my pleasures
—Cousin, it's good—
when the chickens are cackling
co co dac; what do you think, little flirt?

65. Janequin, *Les cris de Paris*

Do you want to hear the cries of Paris? Where's the crowd? Nice hot pies, who will have them? White wine, claret, red wine, for six cents! Hot cheesecake! Get it for half a sous! Tasty little tarts like waffles! They're at the Sign of the Cradle in the Rue de la Harpe. Drink this, drink this! Vinegar, wine vinegar! Red herring, white herring! Do you need a little green sauce? Mustard, fine mustard! Sticks, dry sticks! Old shoes, old shoes! Good hard logs, good hard logs! Cold cabbage, cold cabbage! High and low, I sweep chimneys! Who wants some milk? It's me, it's me, I'm dying of cold! Green peas, green peas! My beautiful lettuce, my lovely chives! Cherries, sweet cherries! Do you need a bit of sand? Very pretty, really lovely! I'm getting some money; I need it! Earn a little profit! The dregs, the dregs. Matches, matches! Old boots, old boots! Plums from Saint Julien! Beans from Maretz, beans! I make husbands jealous! My beautiful leeks, parsley, spinach, sorrel! Peaches from Corbeil! Oranges, oranges! Clean combs, clean combs! Charlotte, my love! Builds an appetite! Reform yourselves, ladies! New things from Germany! Turnips, turnips! Beautiful brooms! Radishes, sweet radishes! Fine Brie! Rosaries for a penny! Chestnuts from Lyon! Parsnips, turnips! Beautiful scales! Matches, dry matches! New wine, new wine! Do you need a little gravel, do you need a little wood? Hot pastries, cold cabbage! Build up your woodpile! Hot biscuits! Hot biscuits! Dry wood, dry wood! Hoops, beautiful hoops! Fine candles! Bundles of sticks! In Paris they put straw on the little bridge. If you want to hear more, go ask them!

(Trans. Honey Meconi)

66. Verdelot, *Madonna, per voi ardo*

My lady, I burn with love for you, and you do not believe it, for you are not as kind as you are beautiful. I look at you and admire you constantly. If you wish to change this great cruelty, lady, are you unaware that for you I die and burn? And in order to admire your infinite beauty and to serve you alone, I desire life.

(H. Colin Slim, *A Gift of Madrigals*, vol. 2 [Chicago: University of Chicago Press, 1972], 443)

67. Arcadelt, *Il bianco e dolce cigno*

The white and gentle swan dies singing, and I, weeping, near the end of my life. Strange and diverse destiny, that he dies without consolation and I die happy. Death, that as I die, fills me entirely with joy and desire. If in dying I feel no other sorrow, I would be content [to die] a thousand times a day.

68. Senfl, *Das G'läut zu Speyer*

Ding dong . . . Now come here, all whom the bells delight, and lend me a hand; pull [the rope] and make some sound! *Ding dong* . . . Don't mix me up, or I'll stop. Come on, hurry! *Ding dong* . . . I don't like tolling so long. *Ding dong*. . . I pray you, tell me what this day is, what happens today that one should so ring? *Ding dong* . . . Such a clangor will drive me mad, I'd rather not hear it. Look up and pull with me. *Ding dong* . . . Pull together in God's name. Whoever comes need not ring long, and may come freely to Matins. Come here, all; come here and help me, sexton. Lay hold who will and can! For the festival, do your best. Therefore, I pray, don't spare yourself. No one will begrudge you. Let's go to it, don't complain, don't run off, lay hold, heave, stretch your arms, work up a sweat. *Ding dong* . . . So, Hans and Paul, swing, don't be lazy. How you wheeze! *Ding dong . . . bong . . .* Don't pull so sharply, so it will ring more brightly. Now it plays fine. *Ding dong . . . mar, mir, maun . . . bum . . .* Now pull together in God's name. Whoever has heard will come. For today's festival, we have rung long. *Mur, maun . . .* Now come, lads, lay hold and ring awhile that the bells may peal. *Mar, mir, mur, maun . . .* Heave with all your might. *Mar, mir, mur, maun . . . ding dong . . .* Look to it and sound out. *Mur, maun . . . Ding dong . . .* So toll well, that it will make a great clang; put your back into it. Bring the offering in while they sing the service. *Mar, mer, mir . . . maun . . .* Pull, dear comrades, who would ring with me. *Mir, mur, maun . . .* Now for this festival, let us all together do our best, grab cord and rope, pull gaily with dispatch. *Mur, maun . . .* So keep together and make it resound as if each of you were two. *Ding dong . . .* Johannes, also begin. Now it sounds well and goes right. So, so, my lad. *Mur, maun . . .* Ho! Now ring together in God's name. Who comes will come. Hans, bestir yourself gaily, that the bell may resound, and see to it that you don't break the rope. *Mur, maun . . . Ding dong . . .* Let all draw near, for this you must do. *Ding dong . . .* Let us summon everyone with our bell, tolled fearlessly. *Ding dong . . .* Even though fervor enlivens the devotions, the bells drown them out on this church day. *Ding dong . . .* The worshippers come, the bells hum, there's much singing and giving; the pastor rises to offer communion. *Mir, maun, mur, maun. . . bum, bum, bum.*

(Modified after the commentary in *The Triumph of Maximilian I*, Nonesuch LP 73016)

69. Claudin de Sermisy, *Tant que vivray*

As long as I live and flourish, I shall serve Love, the mighty god, in deed, in word, in song and harmony. For many days he made me languish, but after sorrow, he made me joyful, because I have the love of a beauty who has a fine form. Her promise is my confidence. Her heart belongs to me, mine to her. Away with sadness; long live happiness. Since in love I have much good fortune.

78. Walter, *Ein feste Burg ist unser Gott*

A mighty fortress is our God, a strong bulwark and defender. He helps free us from all distress that might befall us. The old devil He now treats severely; His awesome force is very powerful and artful; His likeness does not exist on earth.

79. Clemens non Papa, *Souterliedekens*

Psalm 36, *Die boose sprack*

The evil man spoke to himself that he would relish being a sinner. He did not heed the fear of God or bear it in mind. He acted in so deceitful a manner before the Lord that his misdeeds and evil face drew the wrath of all.

Psalm 66, *Vrolick en bly loeft God*

Praise God happily and joyfully, you earthly legion; give Him glory, reveal His praise. To God both great and small will say: Your excellent works are wonderful in the world's fullness, but the godless certainly deny this.

83. Lassus, *Prophetiae sibyllarum*

Polyphonic songs that you hear with a chromatic tenor, these are they, in which our twice-six sibyls once sang with fearless mouth the secrets of salvation.

(Peter Bergquist, "The Poems of Orlando di Lasso's *Prophetiae Sibyllarum* and Their Sources," *Journal of the American Musicological Society* 32 [1979]: 533. All rights reserved.)

84. Gesualdo, *Moro, lasso, al mio duolo*

I die, wearily, in my suffering, and she who could give me life, alas, is she who kills me and will not help me! O, painful death, she who could give me life, alas, gives me death.

85a. Palestrina, *Dum complerentur*

Now that the day of Pentecost had come, they were all saying in accord: Alleluia, alleluia. And suddenly there was a sound from heaven: Alleluia, alleluia, like a rushing, mighty wind, and it filled all the house. Alleluia, alleluia.

Thus when all the disciples congregated together, out of fear of the Jews, an unexpected sound from heaven came upon them, like a rushing, mighty wind, and it filled all the house. Alleluia, alleluia.

86. Palestrina, *Nigra sum*

I am black but beautiful, O you daughters of Jerusalem, as the tents of Kedar, as the curtains of Solomon. Do not look upon me, because I am black, because the sun has looked upon me: my mother's children were angry with me; they made me the keeper of the vineyards.

87. Victoria, Requiem Mass

(A) Lamb of God, who takest away the sins of the world, grant him rest. [two times]
Lamb of God, who takest away the sins of the world, grant him eternal rest.

(B) My harp is turned to mourning, and my music into weeping voices. Spare me, Lord, for my days are nothing.

88. Le Jeune, *La bel' aronde*

Rechant: The beautiful swallow, messenger of the gay season, has come; I have seen her. She flies like a little fly, she flies like a gnat. There she goes, I see her; I recognize her dark back. I see her white belly that shines in the sun.

Chant: Gentle swallow, you come with the loving spring; after summer you go away, you never feel the winter.

89. Lassus, *Cum essem parvulus*

When I was a child, I spoke as a child, I understood as a child, I thought as a child; but when I became a man, I put away childish things. How we see through a mirror in riddles, but then face to face.

(*Norton Anthology of Western Music*, vol. 1 [New York: Norton, 1980], 147)

90. Lassus, *La nuict froide et sombre*

The night, cold and somber, covering earth and heaven in dark shadow, likewise lets sleep, sweet as honey, fall from heaven to the eyes. Then the day that follows, fostering toil, exposes its light and, with diverse colors, clothes and forms this great universe.

91. Rore, *Da le bella contrade d'oriente*

From the beautiful regions of the East clear and joyful rose the morning star, and I was enjoying, in the arms of my divine idol, that pleasure that transcends human understanding, when I heard, after a passionate sigh: "Hope of my heart, sweet desire, you go, alas, you leave me alone, farewell! What will happen to me here, gloomy and sad? Alas, cruel Love, how uncertain and short-lived are your pleasures, for it even pleases you, that the greatest pleasure should end in tears." Unable to say more, she held me tightly, repeating her embraces in more entwinings than ivy or acantus ever made.

92. Marenzio, *Scaldava il sol*

The midday sun burned the arch on the lion's back, its dear lodging. Under the bush, laden more with leaves, the shepherd slept with his flock beside him. The peasant stretched out, freed from work, wanting more rest than food, the birds, the beasts, all men hide and keep still. The cicada alone does not feel at peace.

93. Vecchi, *Caro dolce mio bene*

My dear, sweet love, comfort of my pains, allow me to gaze on your sapphire eyes all the time.

My dear, beloved soul, refuge of my life, allow me to kiss your rosy lips in unaccustomed ways.

You, my dear contentment, remedy for all my torments, allow me also to taste your unripe apples before I die.

And let me hold your ivory breast tightly until we both feel love's messengers in amorous ardor.

(Ruth DeFord, ed., *The Four-Voice Canzonettas, Recent Researches in the Music of the Renaissance* 92–93 [Madison: A-R Editions, 1993], part I, p. 57)

94. Casulana, *Ahi possanza d'amor*

Ay, power of love, how, at the same time, you offer hope and fear to my heart! I ask only for her and death and life, ardor and ice; to suffer and cry, help me perish; then I ask death. Thus as a servant of others I wait happily.

95. Tallis, *In ieiunio et fletu*

Fasting and weeping, the priests prayed: "Spare, O Lord, your people, and let not your people fall into perdition." Between the porch and the altar, the priests wept, saying: "Spare your people."

99a. Gastoldi, *A lieta vita*

To joyful life
Love [Cupid] invites us.
Fa la la.
He who enjoys desire,
if he loves from the heart,
will give his heart
to such a Signore.
Fa la la.

Now happy at last,
troubles driven away.
Fa la la.
Those of us who remain
live in festive fashion
and pay homage
to such a Signore.
Fa la la.

Whoever does not believe in him
has no faith.
Fa la la.
And instead of mirth,
will have the opposite:
the ire and furor
of such a Signore.
Fa la la.